Teaching Information Literacy

35 Practical, Standards-based Exercises for College Students

WITHDRAWN

Joanna M. Burkhardt

Mary C. MacDonald

Andrée J. Rathemacher

AMERICAN LIBRARY ASSOCIATION
Chicago   2003

While extensive effort has gone into ensuring the reliability of information appearing in this book, the publisher makes no warranty, express or implied, on the accuracy or reliability of the information, and does not assume and hereby disclaims any liability to any person for any loss or damage caused by errors or omissions in this publication.

Design and composition by ALA Editions in ITC Century Book and Univers using QuarkXPress 5.0 on a PC platform

Printed on 50-pound white offset, a pH-neutral stock, and bound in 10-point cover stock by Batson Printing

The paper used in this publication meets the minimum requirements of American National Standard for Information Sciences—Permanence of Paper for Printed Library Materials, ANSI Z39.48-1992. ∞

Library of Congress Cataloging-in-Publication Data

Burkhardt, Joanna M.
     Teaching information literacy : 35 practical, standards-based exercises for college students / Joanna M. Burkhardt, Mary C. MacDonald, Andrée J. Rathemacher.
          p.   cm.
     Includes bibliographical references and index.
     ISBN 0-8389-0854-3
     1. Information literacy—Study and teaching (Higher) 2. Information resources—Evaluation—Study and teaching (Higher) 3. Research—Methodology—Study and teaching (Higher) 4. Electronic information resource literacy—Study and teaching (Higher) 5. Computer network resources—Evaluation—Study and teaching (Higher) 6. Internet research—Study and teaching (Higher) 7. Library orientation for college students.
I. MacDonald, Mary C. II. Rathemacher, Andrée J.
III. Title.
ZA3075.B87 2003
028.7'071'1—dc21   2003007074

Printed in the United States of America

07 06 05 04   5 4 3 2

▶▶▶▶▶▶▶▶ CONTENTS

▶▶▶▶▶▶▶▶▶ FIGURES

▶▶▶▶▶▶▶▶▶ ACKNOWLEDGMENTS

*W*e would like to acknowledge the assistance of our families, colleagues, students, employers, and editors in the preparation of this manuscript. We are especially grateful for the patience and forbearance of all of those who helped us through the process, critiqued our exercises, listened to our discussions, read our drafts, and "stood in" for us at events and occasions while we were writing.

*R*esearch on how people learn has been going on for decades. It has been found that each person brings different strengths, skills, and experiences to a learning opportunity. Whether or not they learn anything depends largely upon the individual. The instructor can present material in any number of ways, but it is possible that none of these methods will be useful to everyone in a group of learners. Some students prefer verbal presentations, others respond better to visuals, and still others excel only when they can try something themselves (hands-on). No one method can reach every student. An instructor who wants students to succeed must try to incorporate as many learning methods as possible into his or her teaching sessions or must vary his or her presentation so that all students will have success in some part of the learning experience. There is some evidence that the combination of hearing a verbal explanation and doing a hands-on example relating to the explanation creates a learning situation in which the majority of students learn and retain the lesson.

Students today take a very different approach to research than did their counterparts of twenty or even ten years ago. Gone are the days of the library research marathon during which the student spent hours tracking down the available documents, filling out interlibrary loan requests, and reading in the rare books room. The concept of an assignment that could take an entire semester to complete is outside the realm of most students' understanding. The treasure-hunt approach to research and the satisfaction of finding the research treasure are long gone.

Students of today's universities, colleges, community colleges, and technical schools are rushed. Many have full- or part-time jobs; others have family obligations. Many of today's traditional students have been trained to expect instant results, if not instant gratification, when they want something. Today's students tend to be impatient. They have grown up in a world where fast is good and instant is better. The leisurely dinner is replaced by fast food. The delicious afternoon spent reading a novel is replaced by a ninety-minute made-for-television version of the book or the ever-present *Cliff's Notes*. The long, lazy drive to nowhere on a fall afternoon is replaced by a high-speed tour of the highways leading to the latest hot spot or cold spot for a quick look at the scenery. Students of today want to get the information they need immediately by pushing a button.

Many of the resources students need to complete their higher education assignments are now available in electronic format. They can be accessed via computer, and many times they can be accessed from outside the library building. This creates certain efficiencies for the students. They can save time by working from their dorm rooms, homes, work places, or public libraries. They no longer have to visit the library to find information useful to their needs.

Unfortunately for the future of research, not everything is available electronically. Some information is only available in paper, some information is only available on microform, and some information is only available in the library building. This creates a choice for the student. Most students understand that nonelectronic resources exist. But to use them, one must overcome the inertia involved in leaving home. This could be as simple as a one-minute walk to the library. However, many students today do not live in dorms or even on campus. In today's commuter and distance-education environment, travel to the library resources can be a significant investment of time and energy. It may involve the complexities of getting a baby-sitter, catching a bus, finding a parking place, or taking time out of a normal schedule to get to the library during hours when it is open. The alternative is to stay home and limit oneself to what is available electronically.

By limiting themselves to the information that is available electronically, students limit the thoroughness of their research. It is not yet possible to exhaustively survey the literature of any discipline or topic by using electronic tools alone. Most students understand this, but many do not or cannot overcome the obstacles involved in traveling to the resources they could use in the library.

In an effort to obtain what is needed from home, many students will simply surf the Internet for information and accept anything they find regardless of its quality. Of course, they will usually find information in abundance, but the quality of what they find will inevitably be mixed. Even though time seems to be of the essence for students, they would rather use copious amounts of time sifting through web sites for something usable than make a trip to the library. The faster they can accomplish their assignments, the happier they are, even when the resulting grades are less than stellar.

Many students don't know how the library materials available electronically are different from those they find surfing the Web. Some students have never learned to use a periodical database or an on-line catalog. Unless they are taught the hows and whys of electronic resources, they are likely to use random web sites for their information need, thinking that one source is as good as another.

In the face of this situation, it becomes imperative for academicians to step in and teach students (1) how to find quality information using electronic sources and (2) that tools and resources exist in nonelectronic format. Using those resources may save them time and effort in the long run. Students need to see that the tool that seems to be saving them time may do so at the cost of achieving a good grade because they have inexpertly selected the wrong tool for the job.

Evaluation of resources is critical to the success or failure of the students. Until this is understood a student can only succeed accidentally. The benefit of using library-selected and provided sources lies in the fact that those materials have been written by expert and reliable sources and chosen by expert and reliable professionals. The major evaluation considerations for library materials have already been accomplished by the time the student uses them. This evaluation process is invisible to students for the most part. This, coupled with the fact that so much information is available via the Web, makes students forget—if they ever knew—that not all sources are equally reliable or accurate. For that reason, librarians, instructors, and teaching assistants must be ready to explain this critical difference while training students in the more manual skills of pushing buttons and opening new screens.

It is for these reasons that this workbook has been written. We hope to assist others who are instructing students in the use of the new library tools as well as those who are teaching research methods and concepts. We offer exercises and explanations throughout the book to provide instructors with food for thought as well as ready-to-use or -modify exercises and examples. The exercises can be presented to an individual, a class, or a group of faculty. They can be used as one-shot teaching opportunities or tied together in the context of a semester-long course. Each exercise has been used in the context of our own bibliographic instruction sessions and, more frequently, in our three-credit semester-long course in information literacy.

We hope the content of this book will prove useful and beneficial and provide food for thought as we help mold students of all kinds into information literate learners for life.

CHAPTER ONE ▶▶▶▶▶▶▶▶ Information Explosion

Out in the vast world and beyond, there is an endless amount of information. We have the means to access more information than we will ever be able to process. Today anyone can provide information to others anywhere in the world, on any subject, via the Internet. As the mountain of information gets larger and larger, people begin to suffer from what Richard Saul Wurman calls "information anxiety."[1] As with many other types of anxiety, having some knowledge and training about information and its uses can help reduce information anxiety.

Transmission of information is not strictly a human trait. Many animals, birds, and even insects convey information to one another. Much of this information is very basic: "Go two clicks north to find good nectar." "You are in my territory—get out." "Look out, here comes a tiger!" These are basic survival messages.

In the earliest human groups, conveying these basic survival messages was all that was needed. People lived in small family groups widely scattered over the landscape. Contact with "outsiders" was probably infrequent for these mobile groups of hunters and gatherers. The number of messages necessary to share was small. The speed at which messages traveled was slow. Survival was the main concern.

When plants and animals were domesticated, people were required to stay in one place to care for them. They also had to stay in areas where water and food for the animals was available, so the number of places where people could settle was more limited. This resulted in larger gatherings of people in specific places. Locating in one geographic spot allowed more permanent structures to be built. Domestication of plants and animals also meant that it was possible to have a surplus of food to support the population. A sedentary lifestyle was less stressful for human reproductive systems. The human population grew as a result of all these changes.

As individuals or groups began to "own" things, the need for conveyance of information grew, as did the need for recording it. People needed new messages about geographic boundaries, water rights, whose animals were whose, and how to find the house of a relative or the next settlement. It became easier to "spread" information, and information spread faster because people were closer together. As populations grew, some people began to produce goods as well as food and clothing. Specialists produced tools or other items that helped workers of all kinds do their jobs better, faster, more economically, or just made life easier in general. As more tools were invented, more people were needed to make the tools. Eventually, the demand for specialty goods became so large that the specialists devoted all of their time to producing them. They no longer had the time to produce everything necessary for their own survival. Specialists became dependent on other people for production of things in which they did not specialize. Tools and other specialty items were exchanged for subsistence items such as food and clothing. In some cases, specialty items were sold for money, and the money was used to purchase needed subsistence goods.

During this time of economic and social change, known as the Industrial Revolution, great numbers of people made the switch from farming to manufacturing. A large part of the population began to produce nonsubsistence items. Those products had to be traded or sold for food, shelter, and clothing. To sell the nonsubsistence products required advertising—billboards, catalogs, handbills, and traveling salesmen.

These fundamental changes in the world's economy meant that more record keeping and knowledge of how to use the records were needed. More people learned how to read because it was both possible and necessary, at least for the wealthiest segments of the population. Innovations such as the telegraph and the train sped up communication and made it possible over long distances. It became possible for manufacturers to locate offices in more than one place.

People began to specialize in dealing with the various kinds of documents, books, and other information that were being produced. They also specialized in the analysis and application of the information contained in the documents. The storage of information grew in importance as well. Some information was centrally located. Other information was stored at distributed locations. Information needed in multiple locations required reproduction of that information, either manual or mechanical.

Recently another fundamental economic and social shift has taken place, moving significant segments of the world's working population into service occupations. Storing, managing, manipulating, and understanding information are now the primary activities of many of the jobs performed by educated workers, while food production has moved into the economic background. Information flows quickly via radio, television, phone, and the Internet. With the amount of available information doubling every seven or eight years, the amount of information we will encounter during our lifetimes is almost incomprehensible.[2] This explosion of information has led to a huge increase in the number of workers who manage, analyze, and interpret it. Many have referred to the time in which we now live as the Information Age.

DISCUSSION OF THE MANY AGES OF INFORMATION

Today humans have gone far beyond the basic survival messages of earlier days. Humans have become information rich, at least in terms of volume. It is useful to set the stage for students by discussing these different "ages of information."

Goal: Students will learn the history of information and come to understand why it is important to them. Students will learn to ask questions such as, What can be done with this mountain of information?

Description: The questions listed in **exercise 1** will focus students on the continuum of information. It will give them a sense of how humans arrived at the current stage of information overload and why it makes people anxious. Asking the same questions for each "age" will allow students to compare and contrast the different ages and stages of information.

Tips for conducting the exercise: This discussion should take place in class, using what the students already know about human groups and the kinds of information available during each time period. Creating a picture on a chalkboard or a flipchart may be useful. Draw small circles far apart to represent human groups and their information needs during the Stone Age, for example. Add in water, food, and shelter symbols as students suggest them. The pictures for each successive age should become more and more crowded.

This class discussion addresses ACRL Standard 1, Part 2.

EXERCISE 1

The Many Ages of Information

Stone Age   Agricultural Age   Industrial Age   Information Age

Compare the following considerations for each age:

1. What were the means of communication during this time?

2. What was the speed of the communication? What were the means for "spreading the word"?

3. What was the size of the audience?

4. How much information was transmitted in any one communication? (How big was the file?)

5. What was the purpose of transmitting the information?

6. How important was the need for an accurate and reliable answer?

WHAT IS INFORMATION?

Information is everywhere. It is all around us. There are many mechanisms for conveying information and many reasons for wanting and needing it. But what is it?

This seems like a pretty simple question, but defining the term is not an easy matter. In discussions with students we have found that many have a rough idea of what they think information is, but very few are able to put their definition into words. Several approaches can be used to get students to think about the concept.

Goal: **Exercise 2** gets students to consider the word "information" and its meanings. It will supply students with the "big picture" and make them understand that *everything* is information. The exercise should also get students to ask some questions about how to pluck specific straws of information out of the huge haystack of information that exists.

Description: Through group discussion, this exercise gets students talking and thinking about the nature of information.

Tips for conducting the exercise: The six parts of exercise 2 offer different approaches to the same concept. It is not necessary to have students complete more than one or two at most. For no. 1, distribute index cards and give the instructions verbally. For no. 2, distribute a list of nouns. Ask each student to select a word and decide whether it is or is not information. Have the class argue for or against the designation given. For no. 3, break the class into small groups. Present each group with a set of objects and have them list the information each object might supply. We have included items on our lists that give students pause—dust, a diamond ring, a baby's footprint. Many students indicate at first glance that these are not information. When pressed to think about it, however, students can usually make a list of information that something as simple as dust might convey. Dust might inform you of long absence from a house, sloppy housekeeping, lack of allergies, environmental fallout, neglect, not a priority, lack of time, lack of money to hire a house cleaner. The conclusion to be reached in this discussion is that everything is information. In no. 4, divide the class into small groups. Ask students to list 20 things they think are information. Have Group 1 list their "Top 10" on the chalkboard. Have Group 2 add anything new on their list to the list on the board. Continue through the groups until the list is exhaustive. In no. 5, ask students, in groups or individually, to come up with a one-sentence definition of information. Have them read their definitions to the class. Then ask the class to merge all aspects of each definition into one comprehensive definition. In no. 6, have students find a partner. Each pair of students will select an item from whatever collection of things the instructor cares to assemble. Ask students to use the worksheet to make lists of information that can be gleaned from the item, both actual and inferred.

This assignment addresses ACRL Standard 1, Part 2.

EXERCISE 2

What Is Information?

1. Name anything that is not information and write down your ideas on this index card. Each student will pass his or her card to the student on the right. The student receiving the card will tell the class whether he or she agrees with the assessment.
   _____

2. Select one item from this list of words. Explain why the item is or is not information.

   parking ticket   skeleton   ring   dust   baby's footprint   college catalog
   greeting card   term paper   calendar   transcripts   floppy disk
   motorcycle
   _____

3. You have been given an object or a group of objects. Please make a list of information that the object(s) you have been given might supply.
   _____

4. Make a list of 20 things you consider to be information. Group 1 will record its "Top 10" on the chalkboard. Each of the other groups will fill in or add to the list until it is exhaustive.
   _____

5. Please write a one-sentence definition of information. We will merge all statements into one that the class can agree on as a universal statement.
   _____

6. Take the role of a forensic scientist or archaeologist. (The job of a forensic scientist or archaeologist involves collecting physical evidence and applying a variety of known and sometimes unknown variables to the evidence to determine the importance of the evidence to an event.) Choose one item from the collection provided by the instructor. With a partner, list as many different pieces of information as you can get from the item. The information may be physically present, inferred, or implied. For example, use a piece of antique jewelry. List the following:

   Physical characteristics—style:

   Creator or designer—known, unknown?

   Age of the piece—vintage? antique? modern?

   Gemstones—what kind? how many?

   What other information is physically present, inferred, or implied? (For example, from a broken piece of antique jewelry, you can see that it is of a certain size, shape, and style. You should be able to name the kind of jewelry it is—a ring or a brooch. You might infer what kind of gem is in the piece, the age of the piece, and its value.)

   Precious metals—platinum? gold? sterling?

   Inferred or implied:

   Broken—what part of the piece is damaged? ripped or torn? smashed? broken with age?

   Where was it found—trash? antique store or pawn broker? attic chest? vintage jewelry box or armoire?

INFORMATION ANXIETY

Information anxiety is that helpless feeling that comes with the realization that there is more information than one person can ever hope to process. "So much information, so little time."

Consider these estimates...

> More new information has been produced in the last 30 years than in the previous 5,000.[3]
>
> Close to a million books are published internationally each year.[4]
>
> It is estimated that there are about three billion home pages available through the World Wide Web, which is growing at the rate of 5 million new pages daily.[5]
>
> The volume of printed information doubles every seven or eight years.[6]
>
> The amount of electronic information is doubling every 60 minutes.[7]
>
> A weekday edition of the *New York Times* contains more information than the average person was likely to come across in a lifetime in England in the 1600s.[8]
>
> In one year, the average American will read or complete 3,000 notices and forms, read 100 newspapers and 36 magazines, watch 2,463 hours of television, listen to 730 hours of radio, buy 20 CDs, talk on the telephone almost 61 hours, read three books, and spend countless hours exchanging information in conversations.[9]

Actually, the rate of doubling of print information has stayed fairly constant (doubling every seven or eight years) since 16th-century Europe, when the printing press was invented.[10] So the growth of written information is a historical phenomenon, not peculiar to modern times. What has changed is that we now have computerized information systems that can collect, manipulate, and generate information quickly and efficiently. We have broadcast media, computers, the Internet, satellite systems, and other technologies that provide extremely rapid access to information. These media literally surround us with information. More of us are required to find, evaluate, and apply information than ever before.

OVERCOMING INFORMATION ANXIETY

Information anxiety is a feeling of being overwhelmed that comes when confronting a large information task. This exercise is designed to show students the first steps they need to take to overcome the information anxiety barrier that goes up when they receive a complex assignment.

Goal: The goal of **exercise 3** is to allow students to express their information anxiety and to collectively acknowledge that this feeling is normal—they are not alone. The exercise also shows students that thinking about and identifying key elements of an information-gathering task make it less daunting.

Description: Part I of this exercise confronts students with a huge research and writing assignment, which they are *meant* to think they have to complete. This will cause the onset of information anxiety. Part II of the exercise asks students to analyze how they felt when they received this assignment and to write those feelings down. Part III asks students to consider how to break this large assignment into small, prioritized elements that can be accomplished without anxiety.

Tips for conducting the exercise: Give your students Part I, ask them to read it over, and request questions after everyone has read it. Take questions for two minutes or less. Distribute the index cards for Part II. Allow students five minutes or so to read and accomplish the task. Then collect the index cards and read several of the responses aloud to the class. This usually lightens the students' mood, as some of the responses tend to be humorous and students recognize that others felt the same sense of panic they did. The greatest relief comes, of course, when they learn that they are not required to do the assignment! Get the students to talk about why they felt as they did. Then distribute Part III of the exercise. Ask students to write their answers individually for 10 minutes at most. Discussion should follow, with students contributing ideas they have written. The instructor should emphasize the concept of breaking a large task into smaller pieces to make it less daunting.

This assignment addresses ACRL Standard 1, Parts 1, 2, and 4.

EXERCISE 3

Homelessness in Urban New England: Causes and Effects

PART I WRITE A RESEARCH PAPER

In ten word-processed pages due in two weeks, explain the causes and effects of homelessness in urban areas of New England. Your paper must have a research question, thesis statement, introduction, body, and conclusion. Sources for your paper must be cited using MLA Citation Style and must include the following: five major books on the topic, five articles from appropriate scholarly journals, five high-quality web sites, statistics, and five expert opinions on the topic. You must use the (name of institution) library to do this research.

PART II WRITE A REACTION

This task is daunting. You just got to campus! How can you possibly get this done in two weeks?
Please do the following:

On an index card, write your reaction (your feelings) when you received this assignment. Do not write your name; your reactions will be anonymous.

PART III BREAK THE BIG JOB INTO SMALLER TASKS

1. List below or circle in the text of the assignment any and all words or terms that a student would need to understand in order to accomplish this project.

2. List any and all things/tasks a student would need to know how to do in order to complete this assignment.

3. List any and all questions a student would need to have answered, expanded on, clarified, or otherwise restated in order to accomplish this task.

THE CHARACTERISTICS OF INFORMATION

Some information is *factual*. Factual information is a statement that can be proved. For example, the atomic weight of carbon is 12, or $2 + 2 = 4$. Factual information will always be the same. It doesn't matter how many times you look it up or in how many different places. You will always find the same answer.

Some information is *analytical*. This information is an interpretation of factual information. For example, "Four out of five dentists surveyed recommended sugarless gum for their patients who chew gum." The facts are gathered and used together to arrive at some conclusion. Using analytical information takes some care and thought. If the U.S. Census Report says that families in the United States have an average of 2.7 children per family, what does that mean? Can there actually be .7 of a child? How many families were counted? How was the average found? Who did the calculation? It is important to consider what is actually being reported and how the analysts arrived at their conclusions. See figure 1-1.

Some information is *subjective*, meaning that it is presented from only one point of view. The information represents only one person's opinion or viewpoint. Your personal opinion that the best ice cream flavor is mint chocolate chip is subjective.

Objective information synthesizes information from a number of different sources and presents findings that can be replicated. For example, a researcher reports that she used five sources and that the authors in all five sources agreed on X. Another researcher could go back to those five sources and read about X in order to replicate the results presented by the first researcher. See figure 1-2.

Subjective	Objective
Understood from one point of view	Understood from reviewing many different points of view

FIGURE 1-2
Subjective vs. Objective Information

WHERE DOES INFORMATION COME FROM?

Information often comes from direct observation or experience. This kind of information is known as "primary." The person having this information, or the diary, manuscript, or e-mail where it is first written down is known as a "primary source."

Information does not always come from a primary source. Many information sources collect, analyze, synthesize, and reproduce the information in a new form. The U.S. Census is a good example. Individuals submit primary information about themselves and their families to the Census Bureau, which compiles the information in various categories. The Census Bureau does not report on each individual, but rather reports the total numbers in each category. The information the Census Report provides is therefore "secondary".

Secondary information that is again collected, analyzed, and repackaged is "tertiary" information. See figure 1-3.

Factual	Analytical
Consists of facts, and a fact is "the statement of a thing done or existing"	Interpretations and analyses of facts: interrelations among, implications of, and reasons for
Short	Usually produced by experts
Nonexplanatory	Often found in books and periodical articles
Often found in reference materials (e.g., encyclopedias) and in statistical information published by the federal government	

FIGURE 1-1
Factual vs. Analytical Information

Primary	*Secondary*	*Tertiary*
Information in its original form when it first appears Has not been published anywhere else or put into a context, interpreted, filtered, condensed, or evaluated by anyone else Examples are a professor's lecture, newspaper articles written by people at the scene of an event, the first publication of a scientific study, an original artwork, a handwritten manuscript, letters between two people, someone's diary, or historical documents such as the U.S. Constitution.	Has been removed from its original source and repackaged Restates, rearranges, examines, or interprets information from one or more primary sources Examples are your classmate's notes on a professor's lecture, a newspaper article reporting on a scientific study published elsewhere, an article critiquing a new CD, an encyclopedia article on a topic, or a biography of a famous person. Also, secondary information leads you to primary information Examples are an index to newspaper articles, an index to articles from scientific research journals, or a bibliography of an author's original works.	Even further removed from the original information than a secondary source Leads you to secondary information Examples are a bibliography of critical works about an author, an index to general periodical articles, or a library catalog.

FIGURE 1-3
Characteristics of Information

PRIMARY OR SECONDARY

It is important to know the number of times information has been synthesized or repackaged. Remember the children's game called "Telephone"? Children sit in a circle. The first child whispers a message into the ear of a second child. The second child whispers the message to the third child, and so on around the circle. The last child to receive the message says it out loud. The fun in this game is that the final message and the original message frequently have very little in common. The more people the message passes through, the more garbled it is likely to become.

Unfortunately, this can also happen with more important information. When acquiring information, the researcher should be aware of the nature of the information, and if the information is not primary, should have some idea of how far it is from the primary source.

HOW INFORMATION IS PRESENTED: LET'S BUY A CAR!

Information can come in many different shapes and sizes. The same information can be packaged and shaped to suit the needs of the audience as well as the needs of the information provider. Just as a mother will tell her toddler "hot" instead of trying to discuss the thermodynamics of fire with him, so information providers package information to be appropriate to their goals and their audience.

Goal: **Exercise 4** will illustrate to students the different ways information can be presented and how each one can be useful in appropriate circumstances.

Description: This exercise requires students to address a specific information need and to identify a source that will address that need.

Tips for conducting the exercise: Divide the class into small groups. Present students with the task of buying a car. Ask student groups to identify and write possible sources of information and where that information might be found, using the following chart. When students have completed their charts, ask groups to share their information needs and sources. Discuss the results.

This exercise addresses ACRL Standard 1, Parts 2 and 3, and Standard 3, Parts 2 and 4.

EXERCISE 4

Let's Buy a Car!

You've decided to purchase a used vehicle so you can get off campus. You know you don't have too much to spend—maybe a couple of thousand if you're lucky.
What information do you need to make a purchasing decision?

1. In the first column, list all the information you would want or need to know about the car—things you won't be able to find out until you see it, as well as things you might be able to research in advance.

2. In the second column, list different places you might find the answers to your questions (whom you might ask, where you might look it up, how you will find it out).

What You Want/Need to Know   *Where and Who to Get the Information From*

_____   _____
_____   _____
_____   _____
_____   _____
_____   _____
_____   _____
_____   _____
_____   _____
_____   _____
_____   _____
_____   _____
_____   _____
_____   _____
_____   _____
_____   _____
_____   _____
_____   _____

WHERE DOES THE INFORMATION COME FROM?

To continue the thought process from the previous exercise, students should be instructed to think about where the information comes from and who is responsible for it. Knowing how many times the information has been manipulated or what biases might be reflected in the presentation of the information is very important.

Goal: **Exercise 5** will allow students to prac-tice identifying different types of information from different sources.

Description: Give students a worksheet with the exercise on it. Ask them to write each item in the appropriate box, identifying each information item as primary, secondary, or tertiary and whether it is objective or subjective.

Tips for conducting the exercise: Note that the results from Exercise 4 can also be used for this exercise.

This exercise addresses ACRL Standard 1, Part 2.

EXERCISE 5

What Kind of Information Is It?

For each item on the list below, identify what kind of information it is and put it in the appro-priate place in the grid.

diary   newspaper article   brochure about an appliance

advertisement in a magazine   scientific research article   recipe   billboard

college catalog   best-selling novel   book on the history of World War II

instructions left for the baby sitter

	Objective	*Subjective*
Primary		
Secondary		
Tertiary		

INFORMATION QUALITY

How do students know when they have found information that answers their information need? How can they select the best information from all the sources available? Students must examine the specific information need in order to answer these questions.

What Is the Information Need?

The sources of information and the specific information selected will be determined by the information need. Therefore, an information need must be clearly defined. Most students start with a general topic that gives a general frame of reference or a starting point. This general topic must be narrowed and clearly stated as a question based on the specific information needed. For example, a student may start with the topic "open heart surgery." However, if the student really wants to know about by-pass heart surgery, then information about valve replacement heart surgery will not be relevant even if the information is of high quality. If the student wants information about how many by-pass operations were conducted in 1999, then information about the techniques used for making incisions in the human body is irrelevant. Making the topic specific and framing the search as a question can help identify the appropriate information. Using the specific question, the student will search for information that may answer that question.

What Information Is Appropriate?

Everything is information, but not all information is equally appropriate to use in every situation. So how does a student identify the most appropriate information? A student may find a book on the shelf, an article in a journal, or a web site page. In thoroughly researching a question, a student may find an abundance of sources that will provide information. Sorting through the sources, evaluating those sources, and selecting the information that best supplies the answer to the information need are the heart of information literacy.

How Is Information Evaluated?

When information on a topic is identified and acquired, it is necessary to evaluate it. The evaluation process will tell the searcher whether the information is appropriate to answer the information need. The following questions need to be considered:

What kind of information is it? Information can be categorized to some extent. "Consider the source" is good advice. For example, some information is original or primary. Other information has been filtered, analyzed, processed, or selected by someone other than the original producer. This information is secondary. Information further removed from the original or information *about* information is tertiary. It must be stressed that the further removed the source is from the original, the more the information may have been changed.

WHO IS THE AUTHOR OF THE INFORMATION FOUND?

What credentials does this person have to answer your information need? Who is the expert on your topic? Whose opinion do you want to rely on? Your mom might be the best person to ask how to feed a baby or how to create a budget, but is she the person to rely on for information about open heart surgery? If she is a cardiac surgeon, she may be just the person. The point is, you must think about the author of the information and how likely it is that that person knows what he or she is talking about.

WHO IS SUPPLYING THE INFORMATION FOR THE AUTHOR?

Point of view is another concept to consider. When receiving information it is important to note whether it is subjective or objective. At first, this may not be clear, and it may be other than it appears. Many times advertisers present a product as "the best," "the fastest," "the most reliable," and so on. The presentation of the advertiser can lead the unwary buyer to believe that the information has been presented objectively. However, the advertiser's job is to make the product seem like or sound like the best or the fastest or the most reliable. Advertisers get paid by the manufacturer of the product to do so. One can infer that their presentation of a product is somewhat biased.

In contrast, an agency whose job it is to compare a wide range of things, using equal criteria for each comparison and with no incentive from any manufacturer or seller, will present a more objective view of the products.

WHY IS THE INFORMATION BEING PROVIDED?

The next item to consider is why someone is providing information and who is supporting that person's ability to do so. For example, a doctor who works for the American Cancer Society and a doctor who works for the tobacco industry may provide very different information about the effects of smoking on the body. Both may have equally good credentials. Their reasons for providing the information may be very different.

WHO IS THE AUDIENCE FOR THE INFORMATION?

Are you looking for something geared toward an audience of four-year-olds? The amount of information, the detail involved, and the language used will be different for an audience of four-year-olds than it will be for an audience of adults. Teen magazines may not appeal to members of the U.S. Supreme Court, because the Supreme Court is not the target audience for teen magazines. Again, language, subject, detail, and accuracy may all be influenced by the target audience.

WHERE DID THE INFORMATION COME FROM?

Is the author the primary source of the information? Did the author use other sources in gathering information used in what he is telling you? If so, does the author tell you so and name the sources? If so, are the sources of information sources you would trust? Are they also reliable and accurate? Is there a list of sources provided—a bibliography, for example—to which one can refer to check on details or obtain more information? Or do you just have to take the author's word for it that the information is correct?

IN WHAT KIND OF PUBLICATION IS THE INFORMATION PROVIDED?

Is your information in a glossy magazine with lots of advertising? Is it in a clinical research journal supported by subscription or membership only? Is it from a web site supported by a university or a special interest group?

HOW CURRENT IS THE INFORMATION?

In some cases it doesn't matter how current the information is. If you are looking for the 25th decimal place in pi, it really doesn't matter when the calculation was done. The number should be the same in all cases if the calculation was done correctly. If you are looking for the temperature outdoors today, a temperature reading for last summer is not helpful. If you are performing open heart surgery, having the most current information can be a matter of life and death. Knowing the currency of the information can help you put it in perspective. It can also help you decide whether it is appropriate to use it.

HOW ACCURATE IS THE INFORMATION?

Again, in some cases, precision is not vital. If you need to know in general what time it is, almost any working clock will do. An Olympic speed skater, however, will obviously need an extremely accurate report on the time it took to complete her race. In gathering information, the greater the need for accuracy, the greater the number of sources that should be consulted. This is especially important if the researcher knows little about the subject. In most cases, to determine the accuracy of any information, at least two sources should be consulted.

THE QUALITY OF INFORMATION

The definition of quality information changes with the information need. Some needs can be addressed only by an expert in a particular field. Some needs can be met by casual conversation at the water cooler with no expertise required. It is important to find information of the quality that suits the information need. The expert in a specific field may not be able to supply the appropriate quality of information for the discussion you have at the water cooler, and vice versa.

Goal: The goal of **exercise 6** is to demonstrate the different degrees of quality in information and how each type of information might be useful in a given situation.

Description: Students will find that there are many sources that can provide information about their topic. However, some information may be more applicable than others under certain circumstances. This exercise will give students practice in finding sources of information appropriate to their information need.

Tips for conducting the exercise: Select several information topics for students to work on in pairs or small groups. Define an information need or question for each topic. Collect three sources of information on each topic and distribute them to the student groups. Sample topics might include:

Is a 1998 Toyota Camry a reliable car? Supply one brochure from the Toyota dealer, one article from *Consumer Reports*, and one web site from a Camry enthusiast.

Is using a credit card on-line dangerous? Supply one answer from a merchandiser (perhaps from their web site), one article from a newspaper, and one article from a scholarly journal.

Is Microsoft really a monopoly? Supply one article from Microsoft, one article from a government perspective, and one opinion from a web chat room.

Discuss the findings on as many topics as you have time for. Collecting the information for a large number of topics can be very time-consuming. Think about this exercise well in advance of its delivery date!

This exercise addresses ACRL Standard 1, Part 2 and Standard 3, Part 2.

EXERCISE 6

The Quality of Information

Please identify the information below about each of the sources given to you. If the information is not available and cannot be inferred, leave the space blank.

	Source 1	Source 2	Source 3
Purpose			
Audience			
Authority			
Supplier			
Currency			
Accuracy			
Type of publication			
Primary or secondary			
Subjective or objective			
Quality of information (as relates to the information need) Does this source provide you with high-quality information?			
Usefulness of information (as relates to the information need) Does this source provide you with information that is useful in answering your queries?			

NOTES

1. Richard Saul Wurman, *Information Anxiety: What to Do When Information Doesn't Tell You What You Need to Know* (New York: Bantam, 1990).
2. Wurman, *Information Anxiety*, p. 32.
3. Peter Large, *The Micro Revolution Revisited*, 1984. Quoted in Wurman, *Information Anxiety*, p. 35.
4. University of California at Berkeley, School of Information Management and Systems, *How Much Information?* (Berkeley: Regents of the University of California, 2000). Available at http://www.sims.berkeley.edu/how-much-info/summary.html.
5. Nancy Kranich, "Building Information-Smart Communities," *American Libraries* (December 2000): 5.
6. Large, *The Micro Revolution Revisited*. Quoted in Wurman, p. 35.
7. Katherine S. Mangan, "In Revamped Library Schools, Information Trumps Books," *Chronicle of Higher Education* (April 7, 2000): A43-44.
8. Wurman, *Information Anxiety*, p. 32.
9. Linda Costigan Lederman, "Communication in the Workplace: The Impact of the Information Age and High Technology on Interpersonal Communication in Organizations," in Gary Gumpert and Robert S. Cathcart, eds., *Interpersonal Communication in a Media World*, 3rd ed. (New York: Oxford Univ. Pr., 1986). Quoted in Wurman, *Information Anxiety*, p. 203.
10. Large, *The Micro Revolution Revisited*. Quoted in Wurman, p. 35. "Information Processing," *Encyclopaedia Britannica Online*, available at http://www.eb.com:180/bol/topic?eu=109287&sctn=10. Accessed 12 January 2001.

CHAPTER TWO

Getting Ready for Research

Planning is the key element to producing a good research paper, report, or presentation. However, planning is not a strong suit for many students. It takes time, it takes practice, and it seems irrelevant when faced with a formidable task such as writing a twenty-page term paper. The daunting task of producing that many pages of writing is overwhelming to most people.

There is an anxiety about taking on a big project that is difficult to overcome. Many students have years of real life experience. A growing number of students are older individuals with responsibilities for job, family, homes, and cars. There are many difficult and complicated tasks people take on every day. However, when confronted with a scholarly task, students frequently assume that the process is something new, something completely different from anything they have done before, and they become intimidated.

To make matters worse, students often wait too long to begin their research. Beginners often have no concept of how long the information-collection phase of their project is going to take. As normal humans, students put off tasks they see as difficult and unpleasant. So students may have to rush to find sources, take the first sources that appear, select quotes from those sources without regard to the context in which they were said, and insert them into their own text—where they may or may not support the argument the writer is trying to make.

RESEARCH PROCESS ANALOGIES

Goal: **Exercise 7** illustrates how the academic research process relates to similar processes in everyday life. It builds confidence and allows students to see the applicability of the scholarly research process to reality. It helps to overcome the anxiety and procrastination associated with "doing research."

Description: The following activity is meant to give students practice in recognizing everyday steps to successful research. Have students use an index card to list in detail the steps and actions they would take to fulfill the goal listed on the card.

Tips for conducting the exercise: The instructor should introduce the concept by briefly describing the panic with which a student receives the assignment of a major research paper and follow the uneducated path an imaginary student might take in getting the job done. This should be done with humor if possible. Errors should be exaggerated. Common fallacies should be emphasized. (Oh my, I can never do this—I'll wait until next week. Oh no, I only have a week to write this paper. What do you mean, the library is not open at 3 a.m.?) The exercise should then be introduced with special attention to the analogy aspect—if you can do one of these everyday tasks, you can do research. The instructor should do an example with the class before the teams try it themselves in order to illustrate the detail with which the steps need to be considered. An outline of the research process should follow the exercise so the common factors in the processes can be seen clearly. We have supplied one for instructors following this exercise.

After students have gathered the ingredients and listed the steps necessary to complete each task, have the groups report back to the class with their findings. They will soon notice that whether the task was "Put on Your Socks and Sneakers" or "Plan a Clambake for Twenty," each one has numerous ingredients and multiple steps. In life students accomplish a multitude of complex tasks every day. If they have the proper ingredients and know the steps to doing academic research, they will be successful in their research goals as well.

This exercise works best when done by pairs of students, but small groups work as well. Discussion should be encouraged. While this assignment could be done outside of class, it helps to have the instructor on hand to guide the small groups, keep the work on task, and call time.

This exercise addresses ACRL Standard 1, Part 1 and Standard 4, Part 1.

Here is a suggested list of "tasks to be completed":

Change a baby's diaper

Make a quilt from scratch

Make a pan of lasagna

Plan a camping trip to Acadia National Park

Put on your socks and sneakers.

TOOLS FOR BACKGROUND INFORMATION

At the beginning stages of research, general information is necessary, especially for the beginning researcher who may have little or no knowledge of her topic. A typical example of a general-information tool is an encyclopedia. An encyclopedia article about abortion should provide enough description to suggest narrower categories of inquiry. It might also suggest the size and scope of the general topic. A subject-specific encyclopedia would give more precise information relevant to the discipline in which the topic falls. For example, a medical encyclopedia would emphasize the medical aspects of abortion, while a social sciences encyclopedia would examine social aspects, and a psychological encyclopedia would deal with psychological aspects of the topic. Simply learning that discipline-specific encyclopedias and dictionaries exist is usually a revelation to students new to research. The encyclopedia's main use is to provide an overview of a subject or topic. In addition, encyclopedias can introduce language specific to the research subject area. Knowing the language and terminology of their research area can aid students in designing their research question.

EXERCISE 7

Research Analogies

Goal to Be Completed: (from the index card you received)
(For example: "Open a new bank account")

Please list all of the "ingredients" that are necessary to complete the goal.
For example, (1) cash or checkbook, (2) personal identification, (3) bank's brochure listing types of accounts available, and so on, (4) bank location, (5) bank hours of operation.

  1.
  2.
  3.
  4.
  5.
  6.
  7.
  8.
  9.
10.

Steps necessary to complete the goal:
For example, (1) find a list of banks in the area, (2) pick the one that is most convenient or offers the best terms, (3) read the types of accounts the bank offers, (4) meet with a bank employee to open the account, (5) fill out the necessary forms, (6) write a check, and so on.

  1.
  2.
  3.
  4.
  5.
  6.
  7.
  8.
  9.
10.

The following is a handout that we provide to students
when they are learning the research process.

The Successful Research Process

Keys to Your Success

Research is always a multistep process.

Research is often interdisciplinary.

Think broadly about your topic, then narrow and refine the focus.

Keep a record of everything you find and where and how you find it.

Steps to Your Success

IDENTIFY YOUR TOPIC

The topic is the idea that you are researching. Example: Pollution in the ocean

Brainstorm and concept-map the topic.

Think about and visualize your topic from many different angles.

Note related and interrelated topics.

Note terminology and synonyms that can broaden your searching power.

State your topic as a question. Example: How does pollution affect the ocean?

Refine the question. Example: How does oil pollution affect marine life in the ocean?

Identify key concepts and list synonyms for them. Example: ocean, seawater; pollution, oil spills; marine life, organisms, biology, plants, animals, fish, mammals; impact

List disciplines or subject areas that relate to part of your research. Example: oceanography, environment and life sciences, fisheries, natural resources, marine affairs, biology, aquaculture, business

GATHER BACKGROUND INFORMATION

Get a broad overview of the subject or topic.

Use both general and subject specific encyclopedias and dictionaries.

Get more focused, in-depth, or historical background on the topic.

Use books written in the time period and follow up with more recent information.

FOCUS YOUR RESEARCH

Gather up-to-date, current information on the topic.

Use appropriate periodical information from popular, trade, and scholarly sources.

Use high-quality, appropriate web sites.

Gather in-depth, focused information on the topic.

Search for research studies, surveys, and experiments about your topic.

EVALUATE YOUR SOURCES

Does the author have authority on the topic?

What are the author's credentials?

Is the information accurate for when it was written?

Is there a consensus of opinion on this topic? What are the important ideas?

What is the purpose of the source? How will it impact your research?

Is the purpose to inform, to entertain, to teach, or to influence?

Who is the author writing for? Is it biased in any way?

Has the author looked at the material objectively?

Does the author offer several points of view?

How does the source help answer your research question?

Does the source provide valuable, relevant information?

Does the source answer a part of the total research question?

USING ENCYCLOPEDIAS FOR BACKGROUND INFORMATION

Goals: **Exercise 8** will allow students to begin learning basic search skill strategies and to provide themselves with both background knowledge and terminology in the subject area.

Description: This exercise is an introduction to several basic skills such as key-word searching, using call numbers, and evaluating information. These skills are then used to find encyclopedias that will (1) provide background knowledge on the subject and (2) provide some relevant language and terminology that will help in further defining students' topic ideas.

Tips for conducting this exercise: Show students a variety of encyclopedias, beginning with general and moving on to subject-specific, about two or three different subjects. Examples could include organized crime, civil rights, and nutrition. The subjects should illustrate the range of possibilities available. Use examples that you know are covered well in your collection of encyclopedias. Using a specific article, show students how to identify the author (if the article is signed), the coverage and scope, and the date of publication.

Demonstrate a simple key word search in the library catalog for "encyclopedia AND crime" or "encyclopedia AND nutrition" to help students locate subject-specific encyclopedias relevant to their research topics.

From the bibliographic record in the on-line catalog, demonstrate how to identify what the library call number is for the encyclopedia and where the reference collection is in your library.

The creation of a clear and concise statement or question that will focus the research or project is another task that requires practice. Beginners may have difficulty in selecting the crucial ideas and key concepts in a general discussion or reading. Getting students to think about general topics and how they break down into smaller concepts is something that also needs to be taught. The ever-present freshman paper on "Abortion" is meaningless unless it is subdivided into manageable pieces. It takes several steps from "I think I will write my report on abortion" to a topic that will focus on a particular issue concerning abortion or a particular question to be answered.

This exercise addresses Standard 1, Part 2; Standard 2, Part 2; and Standard 3, Part 1.

CONCEPT MAPPING

Goal: **Exercise 9** allows students to spend time formally engaged in brainstorming the broad research topic. Generating and identifying a variety of specific topic ideas from the broader subject push students to focus on a single idea or to combine several ideas to create a more interesting topic.

Description: Students will select a general topic. In the center of a large piece of paper, students will write their topic word or phrase. They will then write any and all words or phrases they can think of that relate to the central word or phrase. Using boxes, lines, and arrows, students will connect or group ideas that go together, relate to each other, or are subgroups. Students will then select the groups or combinations that have the most appeal for further research.

Tips for conducting the exercise: For this exercise, students may use a variety of marking tools. Pencils with good erasers, colored pencils, felt markers, or crayons work well. Some students have used Post-it notes to jot down initial ideas and then moved the notes around to develop their maps. Each student will need a large size sheet of newsprint paper. There are also computerized software packages that allow concept mapping.

This exercise addresses Standard 1, Part 1.

Figure 2-1 is an example of a concept map on the topic "vegetarianism."

Students are generally open-minded and willing to stretch their minds during the concept-mapping process. After the process, students should have a target topic, a small number of subtopics, and an interest in pursuing an area of inquiry.

Beginning researchers often skip steps that will actually save them time in the long run. One step that can help students prepare to write an effective research question is to consider the disciplines or subject areas that are likely to include their topic of choice. For example, if the topic is "Child Labor and the Silk Trade," all three disciplines of humanities, social sciences, and science are likely to consider some aspect of this topic.

EXERCISE 8

Using Encyclopedias in Research Worksheet

This exercise asks you to find general background information on your subject and language and terminology that will expand your ability to design an appropriate and effective research question.

What is your proposed Paper Trail project topic idea?

Using the Key Word search method demonstrated in class, identify and locate both a general encyclopedia and a subject-specific encyclopedia about your topic.

Which type of encyclopedia is more beneficial? Why?

What is the title of the encyclopedia you chose for this assignment?

What is the title of the article you read?

Who is the author of the article? (Is she or he named?)

What volume is the article in?

What year was the volume published?

Write down the call number from the spine of the volume.

Read the article, taking note of what is covered within it.

List at least five words or phrases that you think constitute terminology specific to the topic you are researching.

Take notes about major ideas offered in the article.

Look for names of other authors and their credentials for further research tools.

Make note of any listed books, bibliographies, or suggested readings.

EXERCISE 9

Concept Mapping

Most people do not think in a linear style when they are working creatively. We think by linking groups of ideas together, "webbing" or "linking" a path to the final subject and topic idea. You will be joining all that you already know with what you learn during your research to build a more complete landscape of the topic you are working on.

Concept mapping helps you create a visual design, picture, or diagram, of the thinking you are engaged in so you can reflect, sort, and refocus the ideas easily. Use this concept mapping exercise to allow your brain to "free-think" along the way to the development of a research question.

PHASE I—BRAINSTORMING INSTRUCTIONS

In the center of the newsprint sheet, write down the most important word, short phrase, or symbol that relates to the subject idea you want to research. Draw a circle around this main idea.

Take a minute or two and think about what you put down on the paper.

Thinking freely, without any expectation of the result, write or mark any and all related words, concepts, or symbols outside the circle. Write anything you can think of that is even remotely related to the topic idea.

Now draw squares around single ideas and circles around groups of ideas.

Use lines to connect these items to the main idea and to groups of related ideas.

Use arrows to interconnect ideas or to form subgroups of ideas.

Leave lots of white space so your concept map has room to grow and develop.

Don't worry about being exact or perfect—don't analyze the work!

PHASE II—EDITING OR REFOCUSING

Think about the relationship of "outside-the-circle" items to the center item.

Erase and replace or shorten words to some key ideas.

Relocate important items closer to each other for better organization.

Link symbols with words to clarify relationships.

What are you thinking about now? How is your topic developing?

Now proceed to topic analysis to further develop your research question!

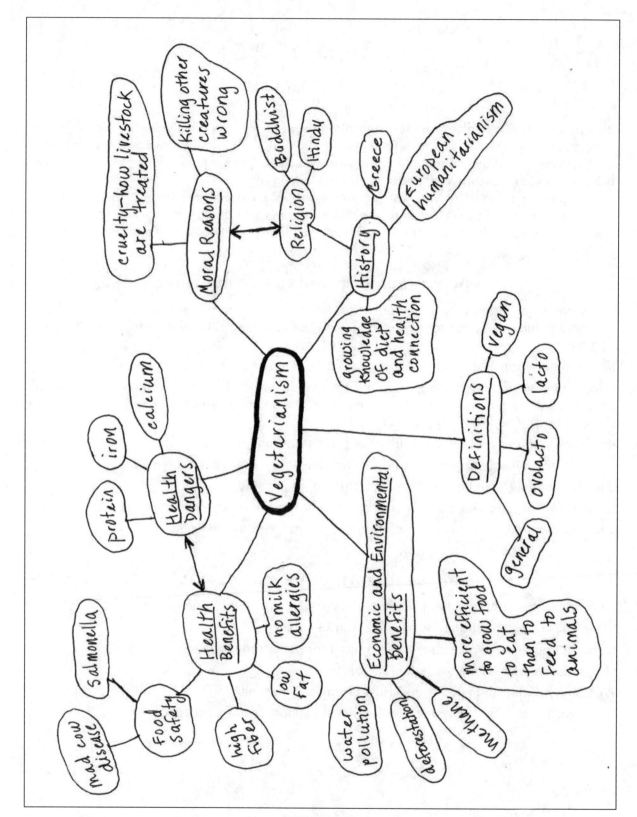

FIGURE 2-1
Concept Map

IDENTIFYING DISCIPLINES AND SUBJECT AREAS

Goal: In **exercise 10** students will identify the academic disciplines and subject areas that will help them answer their to-be-developed research questions.

Description: Give students a handout with a description of the major disciplines and the subjects that fall into those disciplines. Using the catalog of your institution, have the class examine the various departments listed and place each department in a discipline. Then have students use a sample research topic to determine which departments on campus might produce information on that topic.

Tips for conducting the exercise: Have access to print and on-line formats of your institution's annual catalog of programs and courses. This exercise is best carried out as a discussion. Provide definitions of the disciplines from a dictionary such as the Merriam-Webster On-line Dictionary.

This exercise addresses ACRL Standard 1, Part 2 and Standard 3, Parts 3 and 7.

It is necessary to do some preliminary research simply to select a topic. Most students decide on their topic first and then try to find out if there has been anything written on that subject. They are loathe to change or modify their topics, even when they find it impossible to locate materials they need. They are unwilling to use their time to do work that might prove to be of no use in the end. The instructor must show them how this initial legwork will improve the final product and save them time in the long run.

Students are equally unwilling to iterate a change in their topic when they find an overwhelming amount of information. Students may not understand that abortion in and of itself is a meaningless topic. Some work needs to be done to discover that medical and social issues surrounding abortion are two distinct areas of inquiry. The social issues further subdivide into many smaller segments. Until the student does this preliminary investigation, it is impossible to specify exactly what is the theme of the paper or the project to be completed. Definition of the topic proceeds from general to specific, but, again, some practice is necessary to make clear how increasing specificity will help in the acquisition of information pertinent to answering the need for information.

EXERCISE 10

Disciplines and Subject Areas

Now that you have started to gather some topic ideas for your research question, you need to consider where the answers are likely to be found. Before you can know what type of books, periodicals, and web sites to use, you must consider a larger question. What disciplines or subject areas will help to answer the different aspects of your research question? Recognizing the three major disciplines (humanities, social sciences, and science) will help clarify how these areas of knowledge are defined and where your research topic fits in. It will help when you begin to gather information by making it easier to identify some broad-based sources such as encyclopedias.

Review your institution's catalog of academic programs and courses. All of these fields of knowledge fall into one of the three major disciplines listed above.

Into what discipline does each of the following departments fall?

Biology _____

Anthropology _____

Physics _____

Economics _____

Philosophy _____

Agronomy _____

History _____

Sociology _____

In what departments might you find information about the following topics?

Is bilingual education necessary? _____

What is the history of blues and jazz music? _____

Is cloning ethical? _____

Do all of these departments fall into the same disciplines? _____

FORMULATING A RESEARCH QUESTION

Goal: **Exercise 11** will lead students through the process of mentally and visually broadening, narrowing, and restricting the topic ideas that they began to develop during concept mapping. The exercise introduces the concept of Boolean searching and the idea that synonyms and closely related terms can help uncover more ideas on the topic.

Description: In this exercise, students analyze the topic idea created with the concept map and narrow or focus their topic to create a specific research question.

Tips for conducting the exercise: The instructor should provide a guide for students to use as an example to follow. It is also advisable to illustrate how to analyze a topic idea by using a smart board, white board, or chalkboard before the students do their own. Walk them through one or two of the example questions to get them started. As they work, walk around the room asking leading questions to push their ideas forward.

This exercise addresses ACRL Standard 1, Part 1; Standard 3, Part 3; and Standard 4, Part 1.

KEYWORDS AND SEARCH TERMS

Once the research question is constructed, it will be necessary to consider the use of key words and controlled vocabulary. Students frequently do not understand the difference between the two. They may not know how to use those differences to their best advantage. They may not understand that the makers of those search aids commonly used in libraries—indexes, databases, Library of Congress, and so on—do not always apply the same rules or select the same terms.

In using key words, it is possible to use more than one word for the same concept. Students must think about synonyms for their key words. Does the on-line catalog in the library use the term "date rape" or does it use "acquaintance rape"? Does the database automatically link related terms or does it simply return zero results when a specific word or phrase is not found? Is the subject one that might be written about by people of many different cultures, languages, and social backgrounds? If so, such knowledge can be useful in the identification of synonyms that can be valuable to the researcher.

EXERCISE 11

Creating a Research Question

The table below illustrates how a research question develops from a broad topic to a focused question. Follow the four examples down the columns to see how the questions develop. Then use the blank form provided below to develop your own research question.

Broad Topic	Pollution	Commercial fishing	Marketing	Nutrition
Restricted Topic	Acid rain	Fishing and regulations	Nike and marketing	Diets and nutritional benefits
Narrowed Topic	Acid rain in the United States	Fishing regulations and New England	Nike and international marketing	Vegetarianism
Research Question	What can the United States do to prevent acid rain?	What impact do fishing regulations have on commercial fishing in New England?	What are Nike's business practices in international sales?	What nutritional benefits are there to vegetarianism?

Now try out your topic idea below. It is useful to work out several variations of the topic idea to see how it could change slightly and be improved or amended.

Broad Topic				
Restricted Topic				
Narrowed Topic				
Research Question				

DISCOVERING SEARCH TERMS

Goal: **Exercise 12** will help students identify concepts, key words, terms, and synonyms of the words that will become their first round of search terms.

Description: Students will use the instructor-provided Search Term Worksheet that follows to develop a list of concept terms related to the topic idea developed during concept mapping.

Tip for conducting the exercise: We suggest having several dictionaries and thesauri in either on-line or print format available for students to consult during this exercise.

This exercise addresses ACRL Standard 1, Part 1 and Standard 2, Part 2.

As the topic to be researched becomes clearer, more specific tools can be used to identify sources of information about the topic. Both paper and on-line resources should be used. The concept of time sensitivity of some issues must be stressed. For example, the bulk of what was written about the assassination of President John F. Kennedy was written in the 1960s and 1970s. Students may find little or nothing on the topic in the current literature. They must be advised and encouraged to leave the electronic environment if necessary to find information about their topic.

Students should also be advised that there may be parts of bigger works that apply to their topics. A single chapter in a book or a single section in a book of proceedings might be useful, even though the entire book of proceedings is not.

Once the general information has been acquired, it is time to revise the topic. Is it too broad? Is it too narrow? Are there resources that will answer the question? What does the student need to know? Where are the answers most likely to be located?

Information literacy strives to give students a process that they can follow, a step-by-step instruction manual of sorts, to lay out the logical progression of steps to answer any information need. In teaching the research process we lay out the steps for students and have them practice those steps one at a time.

EXERCISE 12

Search Term Worksheet

Search Question: Please write the research question you have developed in the space below: (Example: What is the connection between smoking and depression among teenagers?)

_____
_____
_____
_____

Major Concepts: (List as many as apply.) (Example: smoking, depression, teenagers)

_____
_____
_____
_____

Use the chart below to help you figure out some search terms.

SEARCH TERM WORKSHEET

Concept 1		Concept 2		Concept 3
smoking		depression		teenagers
OR		OR		OR
cigarettes		mental health		teens
OR	AND	OR	AND	OR
tobacco		mood		adolescents
OR				OR
nicotine				youth
				OR
				high school students
				OR
				college students

Search Question: Please write the research question you have developed in the space below:

_____
_____
_____
_____

Use the chart below to help you figure out some search terms.

Major Concepts: (List as many as apply.)

_____
_____
_____
_____

SEARCH TERMS

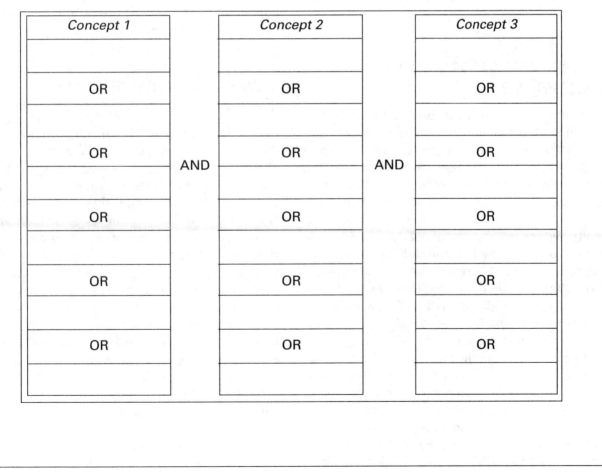

Concept 1		Concept 2		Concept 3
OR		OR		OR
OR	AND	OR	AND	OR
OR		OR		OR
OR		OR		OR
OR		OR		OR

CHAPTER THREE ▶▶▶▶▶▶▶▶ The Chain of Information

As we have mentioned before, we are bombarded with information from numerous sources every single day. How is this information created? Whose creative powers have come into play to produce the information we get?

WHERE DOES INFORMATION COME FROM?

Most information comes to us through a process we call the information cycle. Here is an example. Jane has an idea. Jane gathers information from others about the idea. She talks about the idea with others—at home, at work, at the local baseball game—and gets feedback and input from others about the idea. For the idea to become a reality and for information about the idea to reach others, discussions become increasingly more focused to include experts and other people knowledgeable about the field into which the idea fits. Jane puts her idea in writing. This writing may be a conference paper, a proposal to her boss, a letter to a company that might produce her idea as a new product. Once the idea is in writing, it gets passed around and discussed again. Jane might receive feedback from others to improve or modify her idea or to confirm the idea's validity. The writing might then be translated into a project proposal, or a patent, or a manuscript to be published in a scholarly journal. If it appears that more information is available to be gathered and compiled, one idea might become a book or a group of products.

The next person, John, might read Jane's book and get a new idea, which will start the information cycle over again.

HOW DO WE RECEIVE INFORMATION?

Information comes to us from different sources at different times. For example, as events are taking place, they are usually reported in spoken format during a news broadcast over the radio, television, or Internet. This can happen literally while the event is happening or only moments after. Most of the information in this kind of report is sketchy and includes only very basic facts (who, what, where, when).

With the advent of widespread Internet access, breaking news is increasingly reported in text over the Internet at about the same time as the live broadcasts are taking place. Within a day of the event, its description will appear in daily publications such as newspapers. Again the information will be general and focus on the bare facts, although there may have been enough time to collect some additional information (background about geographic locations, identity of people involved, brief history of a problem).

After a few days, the event will appear in weekly newsmagazines. A magazine article will provide broader coverage of the event, which might include a number of sidebars discussing related topics. There may be more details and even some coverage of the "whys" surrounding an event. These articles are written by staff members who work for the newsmagazine. These authors may or may not be experts on their assigned topics. A newsmagazine does not usually list the sources of its information. Most newsmagazine articles are not allotted enough space to discuss the deeper meanings or possible consequences of a particular event. This type of reporting is usually continued in magazines that are published less frequently, if the event is relevant to the scope of the magazine.

In three to six months, articles will begin to appear in scholarly literature. These articles tend to be written by people who are experts in the field under discussion. The articles can be lengthy and attempt to cover the topic in depth. Many facts will be included along with the analysis of those facts, history of the topic in this particular case and in general, and the possible consequences of the event.

In one to three years, books will appear about the topic. There are many different types of books published for many different types of audiences. All books are lengthy documents. It takes time to compile enough information to create a book. Books can be written by experts or nonexperts. They can be scholarly or popular. They may include a bibliography or not.

Finally, if the topic was of enough interest or had significant impact, a brief outline of the event will appear in a reference tool such as an encyclopedia.

INFORMATION AND TIME

Goal: **Exercise 13** will allow students to understand the kinds of information they might find during, just after, and long after a significant event. It will also provide practice in the identification and location of different sources of information about the same event.

Description: Students will work alone or in teams of two or three. The instructor will pass out index cards on which are written the name of a significant event and its date. Students will be asked to find the first citation for a newspaper article, a magazine article, a scholarly journal article, and a book about this event.

Tips for conducting the exercise: We found that events about ten years in the past provided the best results. With increasing rates of publication in electronic format, it may not always be necessary to identify events that far in the past. Students may need assistance in locating indexes that will cover their event. For example, they may need to go to a paper index rather than using an on-line index with an inadequate date range for coverage. Students could answer the questions during class discussion or as an assignment outside of class.

This exercise addresses ACRL Standard 2.

HOW RESEARCH METHODS DEVELOP

Research has been refined over a long period of time so that it can build upon itself rather than requiring each researcher to start from zero. Before the invention of the printing press, information was located in specific places or with specific people. It was possible for people to share their ideas with others on a very limited basis and scale. Many people did not read or write, and those who did were widely scattered. Information that was written down had to be copied by hand in order to share it with someone not able to get to the location of the original document.

With the invention of the printing press in 1436, the use of information changed over a relatively short period of time. Books, pamphlets, and other types of publications still took a long time to produce, but this mechanical means of producing any number of copies of the same information allowed that information to be shared widely. This meant that existing information could be printed and disseminated, allowing the thinkers of the day to build on the work done in the existing document rather than reinventing the idea from scratch. Printing also made the cost of owning a printed item much more affordable.

EXERCISE 13

Information and Time

You will work in twos or threes. You will be given an index card with a brief description of an event and the date of this event. Working together, find the earliest citation to information about the event in a newspaper, a magazine, a scholarly journal, and a book. Write the complete citations on the worksheet. Then think about the questions below and be ready to discuss them.

Newspaper article: _____

Book: _____

Scholarly journal: _____

Magazine: _____

What kind of publication was the first to supply information about the event?

What kind of publication took the longest to supply information about the event?

What kind of publication would you consider to be the most reliable and authoritative in supplying this information? Why?

Since it was so much easier to get written information, it became much more necessary to become literate. After the invention of the printing press, many more people saw incentive, even necessity, in being able to read.

As literacy and the availability of written information increased, it became increasingly necessary to keep track of the authorship of each document. Knowing who wrote something allowed a researcher to contact the author to ask questions, share insights, or verify the information. Authors wanted others to know that they, and no other, had written some piece of information.

Over a long period of time, it became customary to acknowledge authorship of works cited in one's own publications rather than waiting for someone to ask, "Who wrote that?" The custom of listing works cited became the footnotes, endnotes, and bibliography citations researchers use today. In this way new researchers could show others that they had read all or part of what was already in writing about a particular topic, while introducing new material of their own. Rather than repeating what others said, a new author could simply refer a reader to the other materials of relevance. Needless to say, this saved much time and effort for everyone involved.

For research purposes today, it is usual to start with the most current information on a topic and work backward. But how?

There are several methods for working backward through time to collect information about a topic. One method relies on the researcher having a written piece of information in hand. It may be the current issue of a scholarly publication, a new book, a current newspaper article, or an Internet web site.

In the publication that the researcher has in hand resides a list of sources that the author used to support his or her thesis. This list, which most often appears at the end of a book or scholarly paper, is called a bibliography. It is supplied so that the reader may refer to those other publications. It can tell a knowledgeable reader whether the author has carried out a good search of the existing literature. It can provide the author with credibility by showing that he or she has considered the range of opinion about the question.

The bibliography is also a list of publications about the same topic in which the researcher is interested. By looking at the list of publications in the bibliography of a new book or scholarly article, the reader has a number of other sources about the same topic identified. When looking at a copy of each of the publications in a new bibliography, a researcher can collect additional sources about the same topic from the bibliographies of those books and journal articles. Each of the second set of publications will have a bibliography that will refer to relevant and older materials. The researcher has access to an expanding pyramid of sources of information about a particular topic by moving from the items in one bibliography to the items in their bibliographies to the items in their bibliographies. This chain of information theoretically extends back to the original writing done on the topic.

THE CHAIN OF INFORMATION

Goal: For **exercise 14** students begin with a scholarly work and by using its bibliography work backward in time to re-create part of the chain of information about that topic.

Description: Students will be given a copy of a scholarly article. They will examine the bibliography attached to the article and select two citations. Then the student will locate the publications cited and examine those bibliographies. Two citations will be selected from each of those bibliographies. The student now has four new citations. The four new publications will be located and the bibliographies for those publications will be examined. Two citations will be selected from each of those bibliographies. This procedure might be followed one additional step before becoming too cumbersome.

Tips for conducting the exercise: While it might be possible to do this exercise in small groups, unless one has access to a very large and very comprehensive library (or one that specializes in the selected topic), it may be hard to get an actual copy of the articles selected from the bibliographies. This exercise works best if the instructor selects the citations from the publications before class and already has them on hand for the class. Information could be put on overheads for demonstration purposes.

This exercise addresses ACRL Standard 2, Parts 3 and 5.

It is important for a researcher to know who provided information, at what time in the chain of events, and with how much background knowledge. It is also important to follow the chain of information in order to see how a topic has developed over time, as well as to benefit from the research work already done by others concerning the same topic.

EXERCISE 14

Links in the Chain of Information

For this exercise we will begin by looking at a current article on a topic. Attached to that article is a bibliography. This is a list of publications about the same topic that were used by the author of the current article to create it.

From that bibliographic list, note that two citations are marked. Imagine that you are a researcher. You might scan the bibliography of a current article to find other articles on the same topic. The two citations marked are the citations of interest to you in your role as the imaginary researcher.

> What would you do to get a copy of these publications? (On-line catalog search, interlibrary loan, Union List search, and so on.)

Now we have copies of those two publications. Each of them has a bibliography of its own. Continuing in your role as researcher, select two more citations from each of these bibliographies.

> To obtain copies of these four publications what would you do?

Now that you have received copies of these four publications, you find that each one has its own bibliography. Note that two items from each of these bibliographies have been marked for selection. If you get copies of each of these publications, you will have fifteen articles about your research topic.

> What do you notice about the publication dates as we continue?

> How far back in time could we go using this method?

CHAPTER FOUR ▶▶▶▶▶▶▶▶ Issues of the Information Age

Information has been around for a long time. The issues in using, storing, retrieving, and sharing information have always been with us. Copyright, privacy, and fair use have been debated for centuries. Something like consensus about standard practice has emerged in the United States concerning these topics. However, in the era of the Internet, with all its new technologies, these issues surface again. New formats, new ease of access, and new applications all require that the issues surrounding the use of information be revisited.

QUANTITY OF INFORMATION

Information has become a problem. The sheer amount of information that exists is staggering. The availability of this information to the general public has created a new set of problems. Should everyone be able to see all information that exists? Should everyone be able to use that information, and, if so, how? What happens when the government needs information about an individual? What happens when one individual wants information about someone else? How do you know where "virtual" information comes from? How does one sort out the good information from the bad information? How does one know what is good? How does one find the time to select and evaluate a few sources from among the huge number of possible sources? The mechanisms for delivering information are also expanding in number and in scope. We have moved from the spoken word to the written word and have arrived in a place where we can have information in just about any format geared for any one or more of our senses.

The speed at which information moves is also increasing. Information that used to be transmitted in a haphazard manner by word of mouth can now be delivered specifically, accurately, and in many different formats to any number of people, anywhere on the globe, and sometimes into outer space.

In all this information-centered chaos in the new Information Age, there are new ways of looking at almost every information issue.

INTELLECTUAL PROPERTY

In earlier stages of the Information Age, it was fairly simple to assign intellectual property rights to the appropriate person. You wrote an original story, you put your name on the title page, and it was yours. Today things are not so simple. Information is offered anonymously. Information is offered by groups affiliated with some institution, or on their own. Information is easy to borrow, cut and paste, link to, and modify. Some information is freely available. Other information costs money. How then do we make sense of intellectual property?

Authorship

What is an author? Before the time of computers, an author was usually someone who wrote something on paper. It might be words, it might be music, or it might be mathematical calculations. Today people still become authors in the traditional way. There are also many new technologies people use to create something that makes them authors. For example, in the scientific community an idea might occur to a number of different people who will "toss it around" with other colleagues all over the world via the Internet. As the idea takes shape through this collaborative process, it becomes difficult to identify an owner of the intellectual property. There are really *many* authors. The property belongs to the scientific community at large. This is a concept that is difficult to codify. When information about this scientific idea is published, who gets the credit?

When information comes up on an Internet web site, it is extremely difficult to know where it came from. In a "cut-and-paste" environment any piece of information could come from almost anywhere. It could be that the author of web page A gathered ideas from web pages B, C, and D. Those pages may or may not have identified their authors. The information on web pages B, C, and D may have been swiped, borrowed, or paraphrased from other web pages, other kinds of documents, or other kinds of communications. It is very easy to lose track of authorship on the Internet, where pages come and go, links come and go, and where anyone can post anything they like. Authors would be hard pressed to keep track of their ideas and monitor who is using them for what purpose in the virtual environment. It follows that it is much more difficult to protect the rights of authors in the virtual environment.

Today the word *author* can apply to many people in situations that might never have existed twenty years ago. Is the person who develops a computer program that is stored on the hard drive of a computer an author? Is someone who makes a videotape an author? Is someone who takes a digital image and manipulates it to create something different an author? If all of these people are authors, then they should all be protected under the laws that protect traditional authors. Or should they?

WHAT IS AN AUTHOR?

Many students have never considered what it feels like to be an author. They have never looked at the ownership rights of an author from that point of view. It is common in the current electronic environment to use someone else's work as a starting point for one's own. For example, many nonprofessional designers of web sites are willing to allow others to copy their layouts, color schemes, hot links, and so on. Students will find a web site whose looks they like and copy it, or copy and modify it to suit their own needs. One of the original reasons for the popularity of the Internet was the ability to share, to dispense with the need to reinvent the wheel, and to be able to build on the gains that others made previously.

It is important to remind students, however, that credit must be given to the creators of any intellectual property whether it be ideas or words or programming or images, if they are used in an academic assignment. This is necessary so that others can re-create the trail the student followed in doing his or her research. It is necessary so that individual sources can be accessed for verification or for use by other researchers. It is necessary so that the person who did the original work gets credit for it.

Goal: **Exercise 15** allows students to put themselves in the author's shoes and consider from that point of view what it means to be an author and what an author's rights are.

Description: Divide the class into small groups. Discuss the worksheet questions and jot down ideas. Reconvene the class for a large group discussion. Role-play the plight of an author who discovers that someone is using his or her work without permission and earning lots of money for it.

Tip for conducting the exercise: It is useful to have other instructors who have rehearsed the role-play do the skit for the large group discussion.

This exercise addresses ACRL Standard 5.

EXERCISE 15

Authorship, Rights of Authors, Responsible Use of Other's Work

In small groups, discuss the following questions
and write your best answers in the spaces following.

What or who is an author? What does it mean to create something?

Are you an author? Name some of the things you have created.

Suppose you wrote a prize-winning essay about information literacy. You win a certificate and a handshake from the dean of your college. Then you find out that your roommate sent your essay to a magazine essay contest with his or her name on it instead of yours. Your roommate wins $5,000 and a spot on a popular TV show. How do you feel about what just happened? What can you do about what your roommate did?

Suppose your roommate took only one paragraph of your essay and still won the money and the TV experience. Would you feel any differently?

Suppose your roommate took your ideas, changed the language just a little, and won the money. Now how do you feel?

What is plagiarism?

Why is it important to cite your sources (tell others whose intellectual property you used) when writing or doing other kinds of research? List all the possible reasons you can think of.

Does participation in Napster count as a form of plagiarism or not? Does it infringe on the copyrights of authors or creators?

Publisher

What is a publisher? Back in the day of paper-only publishing, a publisher was a company with employees who oversaw the transformation of a book from a manuscript to a printed volume that could be mass-produced. The publisher had editors, artists, typesetters, printers, and binders to accomplish this task. Publishers produced approximately 100,000 books by these methods in 2000.

Today anyone can be a publisher. All that is required is access to a computer that has access to the Internet. An author can be his or her own publisher. An author may have his or her writing published in paper or electronic format. A writer may have works published by someone unknown to him or her, with or without permission.

Publishing in electronic format has some distinct advantages. Traditional methods of publication are time-consuming, while electronic publishing can take only a matter of minutes. Information published on paper reaches only those who care to buy the published work or visit a library that has purchased the book. Electronic publication potentially puts the writing into the hands of millions of Internet users—at least in theory.

However, the electronic environment is not without its drawbacks. Self-publishing or electronic publishing through someone else may not include the editorial assistance and expertise of a traditional publisher. The layout, the language, and the presentation of the work may receive little or no expert attention if self-published. The millions of potential readers of electronic books may not be required to pay for access to the work, or the content might be copied from a restricted site and placed on an unrestricted site by some savvy hacker. This does not work well for the author and publisher seeking fortune rather than fame. In the electronic environment, it is also relatively simple to cut and paste one author's writing and attribute it to someone else, effectively eliminating any rights the author or publisher might have to the content—at least until the matter is settled through the court system. Again, it is very difficult in the virtual book business for an author or a publisher to keep track of how a work is being modi-

fied and by whom. It is not economically feasible for a publisher to prosecute every misuse of electronically mounted intellectual property, even though protections of the owners' rights exist.

Copyright

Copyright refers to the legal right to reproduce, publish, and sell intellectual property. In many cases the author holds the copyright. This means that the author is the only person who can publish and sell his or her work. An author may give permission for someone else to publish a work without giving up the copyright.

Many times the copyright is held jointly by the author and the publisher. Thus they share the right to reproduce, publish, or sell the work. This is beneficial to both parties. It assists the author by placing the resources and the name of the publisher before the reader. This can result in increased sales for an unknown author, if the publisher has a widely known name and a reputation for publishing good books. Should the author need to enforce copyright by suing, the publisher would be likely to have more resources available for that purpose. The publisher benefits from joint copyright by receiving a portion of the sales revenues.

Sometimes the author assigns the copyright to the publisher entirely. The author may receive a negotiated royalty for every book or journal sold but will no longer own the right to reproduce, publish, or sell the item himself. Any legal considerations regarding the copyright in this case are the sole responsibility of the publisher. The publisher usually receives all or most of the sales receipts and does not have to get the author's permission to change the cover design or the layout.

An institution may also hold a copyright. Just as the patent for an invention created on the job may belong to the company, the copyright on intellectual products created on work time may belong to the institution paying the salary of the author. In this case, the institution reaps the benefits and bears the burdens of holding the copyright.

The Digital Millennium Copyright Act passed by Congress in 1998 was created to extend copyright protections into the digital and electronic environments.

Fair Use

Copyright law is written to protect the owners of the copyright from loss of potential income. There are some provisions that apply to special situations to allow the copyright holders' rights to take a back seat. One of these provisions is known as fair use. Fair use spells out when and how non-copyright holders can use copyrighted material. For example, a photocopy of a journal article may be made for educational purposes as long as the copy is not sold for profit. This allows researchers to do their work without having to bear an unmanageable cost for doing so. It allows research to move forward without having to wait for the copyright holder's permission to copy the material. A teacher may make a copy of something to use as an example in a classroom, to help students learn a concept, idea, painting style, and so on. Fair use provisions are there to allow research, scientific, and scholarly progress to go forward without hampering the copyright holder's right to sell the item.

Plagiarism

Plagiarism is the technical term for stealing someone else's intellectual property. If students cut and paste something created by someone else and do not give credit to the creator, they are plagiarizing. In colleges, universities, and research institutions, plagiarism can cause big problems. Many institutions have very strict guidelines and punishments for those who plagiarize. The electronic environment has changed the way people use information and has made it very difficult to attribute credit to the creator and very easy to borrow the information without attribution.

PLAGIARISM AND HOW TO AVOID IT

Many students, especially those versed in the cut-and-paste world of the computer, do not understand what plagiarism is. Some have vague notions about not using the exact words of others, but for the most part students are unsure about what they must cite. Students may know that they may use information that is "common knowledge" without attribution, but most have no clear idea of what "common knowledge" is. Students tend to think about quoting, citing, and plagiarism only with reference to traditional sources of academic knowledge—books and journals. They need to be encouraged to think about other sources of information and how it is protected as well.

Goal: The goal of **exercise 16** is to identify instances of plagiarism and to learn what can be changed in each exercise to make each passage acceptable to use.

Description: This exercise contains a quotation from a document. The quotation is followed by examples that use the exact words of the passage, that paraphrase the passage, and that use small parts of the passage with and without quotations marks and with and without attribution. This exercise is designed to show specific examples of plagiarism. Students should be able to identify what is missing from the writing or what needs to be done to correct the error.

Tips for conducting the exercise: This exercise works well with individuals, small groups, or as a whole-group discussion. If the group is divided, be sure to bring students back together to discuss each example and to compare notes on their conclusions.

This exercise addresses ACRL Standard 5.

EXERCISE 16

Plagiarism

The quotation below is from an article by Joanna M. Burkhardt. Read the original quotation. Selections 1-5 are ways in which someone might use this information in a term paper. Which of these constitute plagiarism and which are acceptable? Compare the examples that follow and decide whether they are or are not examples of plagiarism. Be ready to explain your answer. Original quotation:

> Library literature offers wide-spectrum coverage on planning and moving libraries. Authors offer visions of what might be, practical implementation suggestions, or explicit instructions for specific situations. Every move is different and offers its own set of challenges. Planning and moving into a new library can be a nightmare with long-range challenges, or a sweet dream of perfect coordination and timing.*

SELECTION 1

Library literature offers wide-spectrum coverage on planning and moving libraries. Authors offer visions of what might be, practical implementation suggestions, or explicit instructions for specific situations. Every move is different and offers its own set of challenges. Planning and moving into a new library can be a nightmare with long-range challenges, or a sweet dream of perfect coordination and timing.

SELECTION 2

Library literature offers wide-spectrum coverage on planning and moving libraries. Authors offer visions of what might be, practical implementation suggestions, or explicit instructions for specific situations. Every move is different and offers its own set of challenges. Planning and moving into a new library can be a nightmare with long-range challenges, or a sweet dream of perfect coordination and timing. (Burkhardt, 1998)

SELECTION 3

"Library literature offers wide-spectrum coverage on planning and moving libraries. Authors offer visions of what might be, practical implementation sugges-

tions, or explicit instructions for specific situations. Every move is different and offers its own set of challenges. Planning and moving into a new library can be a nightmare with long-range challenges or a sweet dream of perfect coordination and timing." (Burkhardt, 1998)

SELECTION 4

Library literature offers much information on planning and moving libraries. Authors offer their thoughts on what might be, practical implementation suggestions, or explicit instructions for specific situations. Every move is different and offers its own set of challenges. Planning and moving into a new library can be a nightmare or a sweet dream of perfect coordination and timing. (Burkhardt, 1998)

SELECTION 5

"Library literature offers much information on planning and moving libraries. Authors offer their thoughts on what might be, practical implementation suggestions, or explicit instructions for specific situations. Every move is different and offers its own set of challenges. Planning and moving into a new library can be a nightmare or a sweet dream of perfect coordination and timing." (Burkhardt, 1998)

SELECTION 6

In the literature about libraries there are plenty of articles on planning and moving libraries. Writers of these articles offer futuristic, practical, or explicit instructions for moving libraries. Planning and moving a library can be a nightmare or a good dream. (Burkhardt, 1998)

SELECTION 7

Moving into a new library takes much planning and forethought. The literature is full of articles of practical and theoretical advice regarding this topic. Each situation is different and must be handled according to the specifics of the location. Creating a new library may be very easy or very hard. (Burkhardt, 1998)

---

* Joanna M. Burkhardt, "Do's and don'ts for moving a small academic library, *College and Research Libraries News* 59, no. 7 (July/August 1998): 499.

When to Cite

How does an author know when it is appropriate to cite someone else's work? The answer to this question is frequently unclear even for a practiced writer. However, in each case an author must make a decision one way or the other—to cite or not to cite. Under the law, the only time it is acceptable not to cite a source for someone else's work is when the information under consideration is common knowledge. An author does not have to find the source for the information "The sun rises in the east." This fact is common knowledge. There are many facts that can be considered common knowledge.

The concept of common knowledge becomes a gray area when we begin to consider the question, Common to whom? It seems fair to assume that every adult knows that the sun rises in the east, wherever they are and whatever their culture. The certainty about what is common knowledge becomes less certain when issues are common to many, but not to all, people. For example, it is common knowledge for adults in the United States that cars drive on the right side of the road in the United States. This may not be common knowledge in other places on the globe. It may be common knowledge for those who use computers that Apple computers invented the concept of computer windows.[1] That information may not be common knowledge to those who do not use computers.

One must be very careful about assuming that what is common knowledge in one's own circle is also common knowledge outside that circle. When in doubt about citing or not citing a source, always cite it. It is *never* wrong to cite your sources.

INFORMATION PRIVACY AND POLICY

Who Owns the Information?

When information is created, the question of who owns it comes up immediately. If it is posted on the Web by the author, it is possible to simply copy or download the file. Technically the author still has the legal rights under copyright law and therefore owns the copyright to the information. The information can be used for education and research as outlined in the fair use provisions of the law. This issue becomes important when others want to access the information.

What happens if the author cedes the copyright to a publisher and that publisher sells the content to an information aggregator? Most compilers of this kind of information sell the information to others. If a company that collects information and gets exclusive rights to that information sells it to subscribers, does that mean that only those who can afford to pay for it can get it? The author has signed away the right to sell or reproduce the information. The publisher has decided to allow only the aggregator (information collector) to publish the information, and the aggregator only allows buyers to see the information. This kind of situation limits information access to those who can afford to pay for it. The increasing number of pay-per-view information aggregators could slow the speed of research to a snail's pace by blocking access to information for those who do not have the money to pay for it.

Who Has Access to the Information?

Access is a very important consideration. Most research that goes on in the world today is based on what other researchers have done in the past. The results of those previous studies and experiments are published in reports, journals, white papers, conference proceedings, and so on. If new findings are restricted in some way so that today's researchers cannot access them with relative ease and in a short period of time, how will research continue to go forward? What about information you give out when you buy a product with a credit card or order something from a catalog? Who has the right to the use of that information? Unless you give explicit instructions otherwise, the credit card companies and catalog companies can use the information you give them, or they can sell that information to others who can then contact you or learn about your shopping preferences, annual income, credit rating, and so on.

Goal: **Exercise 17** will show students how easy it is to get personal information electronically. They will also find out that people's "private" information may not be as private as they think.

Description: Using the anywho.com web site, students will look up their own names, the name of a friend or family member, or the name of someone selected by the instructor. Students will gather all the free information they can about this person. They will also find what other information is available about this person if they are willing to pay for it.

Tips for conducting the exercise: It is useful for the instructor to have a list of names that have been looked up ahead of time to ensure that there is a listing relevant to the students. For example, look up the name of the Provost of the University, the Director of the Library, the local television news anchor, and so on. If students do not find a listing for themselves, the instructor can provide a name that will provide the desired results.

This exercise addresses ACRL Standard 5.

How does the electronic environment change an individual's right to privacy?

If an individual does most of his or her research, correspondence, banking, or buying and selling on-line, who has the right to see those transactions and under what circumstances? Hackers have been tracked down using their Internet service provider's records of transactions. This is something akin to a phone tap on the telephone of a suspect. Used for law enforcement purposes when probable cause has been shown, most people would not find this situation troubling. However, what about the "cookies" that web sites place on your computer when you access those sites? What do those cookies actually do? What can outsiders do with the cookies on your computer? What about the situation during which your computer is always connected to the Internet via a DSL? Can the information residing on your computer be tapped without probable cause and without a court order? Can companies track what and from whom you have bought things? Can "Big Brother" tell what sites you are visiting? Who has access to

information about what you have accessed on-line? When you agree to make your computer a server in order to get a service (like Napster, for example), what information that resides on your computer is available for outsiders to look at?

PRIVACY ISSUES

The issue of privacy is very complex and subject to opinion and interpretation. Many people are unaware that information about them is gathered from many different electronic sources. They may not know that using a particular Internet site or tool may authorize the site owners to use the information collected in various ways. Some people do not want any information about themselves available in a public forum. Others have little or no concern in this regard. The events of September 11, 2001, and the perceived need for agencies to be able to access personal information more easily complicate the issue even further. If having specific information available to the government for reasons of national security is necessary to keep everyone safe, is it better to give up some amount of privacy?

Goal: The goal of **exercise 18** is to make students aware of the issues surrounding the topic of privacy and the complexity of coming to any conclusions as to where the rights of the individual stop and the needs for national security, or commerce, or other group needs begin.

Description: Have students log onto the EPIC web site. Select one of the listed topics. Have the students explore the topic and then discuss the issue as a whole. For example, have students look at the following web file at the EPIC site: http://www.epic.org/privacy/internet/cookies/.

Individually or in small groups, have students examine the issue raised regarding cookies. Bring the group back together and discuss the privacy issue and its problems as a large group.

Tips for conducting the exercise: Assign pairs of students to explore an issue at the EPIC site, and, when the large group is brought back together, have each duo present what they learned to the rest of the group.

This exercise addresses ARCL Standard 5.

EXERCISE 17

Privacy and the Internet

Go to the web site www.anywho.com/. Type in your own name. If there are no results for your name, use the name of someone in the business community in your area. Select a listing.

How many things can you find out about the person whose name you selected?

What name did you search?

How many listings were there for that name?

After selecting one listing, what were you able to find out about that individual with no cost to you?

What would you be able to find out if you were willing to pay for the information?

How much would it cost to access the public records of the person you looked up?

How do you feel about having this type and amount of information available electronically to anyone in the world?

EXERCISE 18

Your right to privacy

Go to the Electronic Privacy Information Center web site at: http://www.epic.org/. Examine the issues listed on this site. Go to the link for Privacy in the EPIC Policy Archives. Select one topic from the A-Z list of privacy topics. Examine the issue as presented. Write down the important points, the pros and cons, and the concerns regarding this topic. Report back to the class what you learned.

What is the issue?

Why is it a problem?

How does it infringe on the average person's right to privacy?

What is being done about it?

Preservation of the Human Record

Preservation is a very serious consideration in the electronic world of today. Many records that used to be kept on paper have been moved to the electronic environment. What happens to older records or writings in the electronic environment? What procedures are in place to preserve electronic documents for the historic record? For example, e-mail has replaced letters sent by U.S. mail in many instances. Only recently has anyone thought how to preserve those correspondences which might be of value to history or to law. During the Iran Contra investigations, the President George H. W. Bush White House sought to destroy all the e-mail for that administration as part of the cover-up. The issue was taken to court only hours before the administration left office. Up to that point no one had considered e-mail as part of the public record. Yet some very important communications took place via e-mail, and they could have been lost to history with one delete message to the computer. Fortunately, the judge who considered the case found that e-mail was part of the public record and acted in time to save those e-mails from destruction. But how were they saved? Are the original computers on which they reside in a big warehouse somewhere? Were the messages downloaded onto a super computer somewhere? What will ensure that we will be able to read those messages decades from now when the new technology of that era may look nothing like the technology of our own era or that of the Bush administration?

Many U.S. government documents are now only available in electronic format. This may decrease the amount of paper used in the production of these documents. However, this practice does raise a new difficulty. How will people who don't have computers or who don't have access to computers be able to obtain these documents? Will information access be limited to the rich or to those who have a computer available to them?

What Needs to Be Saved?

Do all e-mails need to be saved? Are all web sites valuable to history? Who will decide? Where will they be kept? Who will be able to look at them? A web site about what happened in the daily life of an adolescent teenager who just moved to a new city might not be of vital interest right now, but what about researchers of the future who want to look back to the beginnings of the electronic age to see how it affected people in their daily lives? Researchers today are seeking out diaries and journals of people who were among the first settlers of the western United States to get their views of what was important and meaningful and eventful in their lives. Might not researchers be interested in the same kinds of things on the new electronic frontier?

Web sites come and go at an amazing rate, many lasting only a few weeks or months. As this is the case, how will information be saved? Will there be a repository of abandoned web sites where all inactive sites can be stored for future use? Is it the job of the government to provide a place where it will be saved? What about international correspondence, web sites, and other electronic creations? Will there be a giant computer somewhere in which all these data can be stored? Will authors have any say over who stores their information?

How Will People Access What Is Saved?

What equipment will be used to keep access to these electronic files available? There was a U.S. Census that was placed on computer disks which are now unreadable because the hardware to read them no longer exists. Will everything that is happening in today's electronic environment be lost when the next new technology comes along and replaces the floppy disk, the CD, the DVD, and so on?

Who Is Responsible for Keeping, Storing, and Providing Access to Today's Information?

Will it be necessary to create a new government agency to collect, preserve, and provide access to information that is only available in electronic format? Will libraries become the repository of these new formats for information? What will become of information from other countries? Will a global mass of information be kept on the international space station? Will the government decide what is worth keeping and what is to be thrown away? How will those decisions be made?

It is clear that there are many questions about electronic information that cannot yet be answered. It is very possible that valuable information will be lost now and in the future due to a lack of methods for collecting, storing, and accessing it. Some information will be saved by luck, some by law, and some by stubborn souls who will not allow information to simply disappear. At this moment we have many more questions than we have solutions to the issues of the Information Age.

NOTE

1. *Encyclopedia of Computers and Computer History*, edited by Raúl Rojas (Chicago: Fitzroy Dearborn, 2001), v. 2, p. 828.

CHAPTER FIVE

Books and Catalogs

Today's students are likely to begin a research project by searching for information on the Internet. They will use other information sources and formats only if the Internet fails them. Without a helpful introduction to the value and use of books in research, students might easily glide right by the bookshelves, assuming that the information in books is old and therefore useless. Students need to practice finding and evaluating monographic information so that they can develop a command for when and how to use books in research.

Before students can evaluate the content or begin to appreciate the organizational structure of the book, they must be able to actually find a book in the library at your institution. Some students are not familiar with the size or organizational layout of an academic library. Even though many students are adept at surfing the Web, most seem to find it difficult to use an on-line library catalog. This may be because many students have hidden anxiety about using library research tools and the catalog!

Catalogs help people to identify and find things. There is a catalog for almost any product or service that one can imagine. Paging through a clothing catalog or surfing a web-based catalog to find a product or service is a familiar activity for today's students, but transferring that skill to the use of the library catalog may require instruction.

WHAT *IS* A CATALOG, WHAT'S *IN* A CATALOG?

Goal: In **exercise 19**, students will gain an understanding of what kinds of information catalogs provide and how catalogs can differ from one another.

Description: Small groups of students will examine multiple catalogs. They will discuss several questions that will help them identify the uses and the limitations of the catalogs. Finally, students will compare the catalogs with the library catalog to identify the similarities and differences.

Tips for conducting the exercise: Gather a wide variety of catalogs: garden, sports equipment, clothing, book club, record club, music store, museum, art gallery, and university or college catalogs. Have at least two different types of catalogs for each small group in the class. Also provide students with Internet access to your library catalog or print several bibliographic records from your catalog for students to examine.

This exercise addresses ACRL Standard 1, Part 2 and Standard 2, Part 1.

Catalogs allow us to know that an item exists by listing and describing attributes that can give us clues to its value to our research. However, as researchers, we need to obtain far greater informational detail to truly understand the value of each item that is listed within the catalog. To accurately evaluate an item from the library catalog, it is necessary to have access to its contents.

EXERCISE 19

Group Discussion:
What *Is* a Catalog? What's *in* a Catalog?

Look up a dictionary definition of the word "catalog."

Name any catalogs that you are familiar with.

Make a list of all the catalogs mentioned on a chalkboard or flip chart.

What kinds of information do the catalogs offer?

How are the catalogs organized?

What similarities are there in the way that this information is offered?

What do the catalogs have in common?

What do they all do for the reader?

After five minutes, record your groups' ideas on the board or flip chart, organizing them into categories as you go along: type of item, product name, classification and identification code, size, color, availability, cost.

Compare the library catalog record printouts handed out to the item records in other catalogs and answer the questions below.

Do all types of catalogs provide similar information?

What does that tell us about our library's catalog?

What can we use it for?

Identify and list what the catalogs *do not* do.

Would you be able to accurately evaluate an item from a catalog, based on the catalog record?

Could you try it on for size?

Could you taste it?

Could you be sure that the product actually matches the information needed?

FINDING BOOKS

The first few attempts at using a college or university library can be a difficult experience for many students. There is a reticence to embarking on the adventure when faced with both the size of the library building and the size of the collections in higher education libraries.

FREE-RANGE SEARCHING IN THE COLLEGE LIBRARY

Goal: Students will gain an appreciation for and recognition of the importance of the Library of Congress Classification System in **exercise 20**.

Description: The instructor will provide each student or pair of students with an index card listing the title and author of a book available in the library. Students will search for the book without using the catalog or the library staff. They may utilize any signage available and their common sense! After ten minutes, the class regroups to discuss the results of the search. This discussion is a good lead-in to learning how to use a library catalog.

Tips for conducting the research: Check the library catalog to identify monographs that are available. On the index card for each item to be searched, list only the complete title of the book and author's name. It is best to use books with somewhat ambiguous titles so that the subject is not overly obvious.

This exercise addresses ACRL Standard 1, Parts 1 and 4.

EXERCISE 20

Free-Range Searching

The index card you have been given contains basic information about a book in this library. The card lists the author's name and the complete title of the book. Your task is to use this information to find this exact book in the library and bring it back to the class, without using the catalog or any library personnel. You have ten minutes to search for and retrieve the book you have been assigned. At the end of the time period, return to the class with or without the book in hand. At that point, we will discuss the results of everyone's "free-range" search.

How did it feel to be searching with so few clues?

Did you learn or notice anything helpful about the library while they were searching?

Did you see anything that could provide clues to help you to find your book?

What other information do you think you need to know to have a more successful search?

THE BIBLIOGRAPHIC RECORD

Library catalogs include all the necessary information to describe an item, tell us if our library owns it, and if so, how we can find it. Most students are not enamored of the details of the MARC record, nor do they desire to understand the intricacy with which librarians build bibliographic records to provide individual record access to unique titles. However, the more that students know about the details of the bibliographic record, the more time they will save in their hunt for appropriate research materials in the library.

BUILDING A PERSONAL BIBLIOGRAPHIC RECORD

Goal: Students will gain understanding of the elements included in a library catalog bibliographic record in **exercise 21**.

Description: Explain that library catalogs are made up of a large number of bibliographic records.

Each record contains information about a unique item in the library's collection. Identify and explain the elements of the bibliographic record. After a brief introduction to parts or fields of the bibliographic record, ask students to use their own unique personal information to complete a bibliographic record about themselves, identifying and relating the elements of the format to reflect their own information.

Tips for conducting the research: Use a complete bibliographic record that the students can use as a model for creating their own bibliographic record. Use a record for a title many students will have read in high school, such as *Catcher in the Rye* by J. D. Salinger or *The Color Purple* by Alice Walker. It may be helpful to create a blank bibliographic record form based on your library's catalog software system for the students to use.

This exercise addresses ACRL Standard 1, Part 2 and Standard 2, Part 1.

EXERCISE 21

Build-It-Yourself: Your Own Bibliographic Record

Using your knowledge of the parts and fields of a bibliographic record, use the printout provided by the instructor as a model to create a bibliographic record for yourself. Use all of the fields included in the three major parts of the record: bibliographic, location, and descriptive.

Were you able to completely and accurately describe yourself using the bibliographic record format?

Do you see any limitations to the format?

Does having a bibliographic record for an item tell a researcher enough to judge the value of the work to them as a researcher?

Does there seem to be a most important part of the record? If so, what would it be?

It doesn't take long for students who are looking for research materials in any library to agree that knowing the call number of a particular item is very important. Assuming their previous experience has been in using the Dewey Decimal System, the Library of Congress Classification System will seem like another enormous hurdle to jump. To a new library researcher, the Library of Congress Classification System, with its twenty broad areas of knowledge, classes, and subclasses, can sound like a college course in itself! There are several quick methods to help students learn to use the LC System including library-created guides and handouts; locally made and proprietary on-line computer tutorials; and the "book truck rodeo."

READING LIBRARY OF CONGRESS CALL NUMBERS

Goal: In **exercise 22** students will be introduced to the Library of Congress Classification System.

Description: The instructor will use a handout or web site to teach students how to read the LC Classification numbers or call numbers. Students will then apply this knowledge to two groups of books in a game setting where they may earn a small prize for accuracy and speed.

Tips for conducting the exercise: For each small group of three or four students, provide a book truck with one shelf of books (approximately twenty) from a wide range of LC classifications. For rodeo prizes, you might award extra credit points or hard candies. Be sure to have a watch with a second hand or a timer available for this exercise so you can identify the winner of the rodeo.

This exercise addresses ACRL Standard 2, Parts 2 and 3.

It is helpful to do a quick introduction to the catalog using an on-line "walking tour" to familiarize students with the look and feel of the catalog system. Design the walking tour to cover both basic and advanced catalog search skills as time

---

EXERCISE 22

Book Truck Rodeo!

Warm Ups: Practice putting the books on your assigned book truck in order as they would be on a library shelf. When you feel certain that the books on your truck are in the correct order, ask the instructor to check and approve your work. If necessary, practice once or twice more until you are comfortable with the concepts of the LC call number system.

The Rodeo: Switch book trucks with another group in the class. Now you will be timed for accuracy and efficiency! Put the "new" book truck in order as accurately and as quickly as you can. Your instructor will act as timekeeper. First group to complete their shelving accurately wins the prize!

---

allows. Also consider using this method to provide opportunities for students to explore other features that your library catalog offers, such as limiting, scoping, and restricting searches.

Today's web-savvy students will try searching the library catalog using natural language and keyword searches. The idea of using formalized subject terminology is relatively unknown to them. It takes time for them to recognize that in research there are formalized language systems such as the Library of Congress Subject Heading System and database descriptors that help ferret out the information they need.

CONTROLLED VOCABULARY AND SUBJECT HEADINGS

Goal: In **exercise 23** students will understand the use of a controlled vocabulary system and improve their search results when using the library catalog.

Description: Students will search the library catalog for an assigned term or phrase, using the keyword search function. They will note the total number of items found. They will identify the LC Subject Headings in some of the records for the titles they find. They will select one or two Subject Headings and do a search using the Subject Search function. The results of the two searches will then be compared.

Tips for conducting the exercise: This exercise is best done with pairs of students or in a small group setting. Topics we have used for this exercise include binge drinking among college students, ocean dumping, Jim Crow, Vietnam War, World War II, nursing careers, legalization of marijuana in the United States, Samuel Clemens, Italian cooking.

This exercise addresses ACRL Standard 1, Part 1 and Standard 2, Part 2.

EXERCISE 23

Using Key Words to Identify Subject Headings

You will receive an index card with a word or phrase on it.
Search the library catalog for the topic on the index card
by using the keyword or "word search" function.

How many items did you find listed? (Write the number in the space below.)

Browse through the titles. Are all the titles listed relevant to your topic?

Go to the full bibliographic record for two or three titles from the list. Find the Subject field in the bibliographic record for each item and examine the Library of Congress Subject Headings listed. In the space below, find and record all of the Library of Congress Subject Headings for each book. Be complete.

(Continued)

Which Subject Heading do you think best describes the topic on your index card? You may feel that there is more than one; if so, select more than one.

Use the Subject search in the library catalog and type in one of the Subject Headings you selected above. How many Subjects were found?

Does the catalog provide any "Related Subjects?" If so, list one or two.

In the space below, note one or two subdivisions of your Library of Congress Subject Headings. For example, "the main LCSH is 'Electronic Commerce,' but in searching for that subject heading, I also see 'Electronic Commerce—Asia' and 'Electronic Commerce—Economic Aspects.'"

How many items were found under the main LCSH you typed in? Look at the titles retrieved. Are the titles listed relevant to your topic?

Overall, which search method ("Word Search" or "Subject" search) produced more *focused, effective* results?

Why do you think this was the case? Be able to explain.

EVALUATION

In research, each of the sources that students select must be evaluated for a variety of criteria: authorship, credibility, accuracy, reliability, currency, timeliness, scope, coverage, and relevance. Students must practice the application of evaluation criteria to each source, rather than simply using those sources that they find first or that come to hand most easily. An easy first step in learning to apply evaluation criteria is to evaluate several books on the same subject or topic and compare the results.

EVALUATING BOOKS

Goal: In **exercise 24** students will practice applying evaluation criteria to research materials.

Description: In small groups, students will apply evaluation criteria to several different books on the same topic and answer questions about the process. The groups will report back to the class on their findings. Contrasts, similarities, and comparisons will be observed.

Tips for conducting the search: For each group of students, gather three books on a topic. Each group should have a different topic to better illustrate that evaluation criteria can change based on the material. Some suggestions for topics are nuclear energy, climate change, and drug abuse. One of the books could be "perfect" (based on the criteria) for the group's assigned topic, one could be outdated, and one could be from an unidentifiable source. This exercise is best done by pairs of students or small groups.

This exercise addresses ACRL Standard 3, Part 2.

Convincing students that *they themselves* are the filters of the information that they choose to use and include in their research is no easy task. Teaching students to recognize when information is valuable for their information needs—and when it isn't—is an important skill that will stay with them throughout their lives.

ANNOTATED BIBLIOGRAPHY OF BOOKS

Goal: In **exercise 25** students will gain practice in citation style, annotating and briefly evaluating books as they relate to a specific information need.

Description: The instructor provides instructions and a guide for students to follow. Students will use the library catalog to find five books on a preapproved topic. Students will write citations, annotations, and brief evaluative comments about each of the books selected.

Tips for conducting the research: Show students how to identify and review the parts of a book used for annotating: table of contents, index, preface or introduction, and book arrangement. Supply a sample citation, an example annotation, and an evaluative criteria chart.

This exercise addresses ACRL Standard 1, Parts 1, 3, and 4; Standard 2, Parts 1, 2, 3, 4, and 5; Standard 3, Parts 1 and 2; Standard 4, Parts 2 and 3; and Standard 5, Parts 1 and 3.

Providing students with a variety of hands-on opportunities to explore the library's catalog allows them to become effective searchers able to find and locate books in the library. Understanding that finding the right books need not be a "needle in a haystack" situation goes a long way to building research confidence in college students.

EXERCISE 24

Evaluating Books for Value

You have been given three books to evaluate. They are all about the same topic, but there is no guarantee that all three are quality sources of information. Your job is to use the evaluative criteria listed below and to take notes on how each source answers the evaluation criteria. In fifteen or twenty minutes, your group will report back to the class with your findings on the three information sources.

First—Review the Bibliographic Information:

Author(s): What is their authority or credibility? Do they have the expertise to say or write what they did? What is their educational background? What is their career experience?

Date of Publication: When was the source published? Is the book a recent publication or is the information out-of-date for the topic?

Edition or Revision: Is this book a first edition? If it is a second or multiple edition copy, can you tell how it is different from earlier editions?

Publisher: Who is the publisher? Is it a university press? Do you recognize the publisher?

Next—Do a Content Analysis:

Purpose: Why was this written? What is the intent of the author? Who is the intended audience? Who is the author trying to inform or influence?

Relevance: Is the material appropriate and useful for your research? Does it answer all or part of your research question? Can it be used for background or to focus on a specific area?

Scope and Coverage of Material: Can you tell if the author intends to provide comprehensive coverage of a subject or topic? What are the limitations of the information? What time period is covered? Where was it published? Does geographical area impact the informational content?

Objectivity: Do you see any evidence of bias, propaganda, or a strong persuasive argument? Is the material viewed from more than one point of view? Does it contain substantiated fact?

Writing Quality: Is it clear to you what the author intends to share and express? Is there evidence of clear organization and writing? Has it been well researched? Are there any obvious pieces of information missing?

Writing an Annotated Bibliography of Books

This exercise contains many research skills that you will need to be an effective researcher in college: finding books, citing sources, summarizing information, and evaluating materials for your research need. A bibliography is a list of sources that were used as resource material for the paper or project at hand. For this exercise:

Search the library catalog for your topic.

Find five books on your topic and retrieve them.

Examine the books you found and determine whether or not they are appropriate for your topic.

If they are not appropriate, go back to the library catalog until you have identified five appropriate books.

Print out the full bibliographic record from the catalog for each of the five books.

Next, photocopy the title page of each of the books.

On a separate piece of paper, following the example provided below, type the citation for each book, providing all relevant information. The citation should follow this format:

Lastname-Author, Firstname. *The Title of the Book is capitalized and put in italics: The Subtitle is also included.* City: Publisher, Year.

Beneath each citation, using your own words, type an annotation. An annotation is a brief descriptive and evaluative note that provides enough information about the book so a person can decide whether or not to consult the book.

To write an annotation, you will comment, in paragraph form, on the following elements:

Content—What's the book about? Is it relevant to your research?

Purpose—What's it for? Why was this book written?

Methods used to collect data—Where did the information come from?

Usefulness—What does it do for your research?

Reliability—Is the information accurate?

Authority—Is it written by someone who has the expertise to author the information?

Currency—Is it new? Is it up-to-date for the topic?

Scope/Coverage/Limitations—What does it cover? What does the author state that he or she will cover? What doesn't the book provide that would be helpful?

(Continued)

Writing an Annotated Bibliography of Books (cont'd)

Arrangement—How is the book organized? Are there any special "added-value" features?

Ease of use—Can a "real person" use this book? What reading level is the book?

Here is a sample citation and annotation to get you started:

List, Carla J. *Information Research*. Dubuque, Ia.: Kendall/Hunt Publishing Co., 2002.

In this book, Carla List, an award-winning teacher and librarian, defines and describes information and provides step-by-step instruction on doing research. In seven chapters, she covers the organization of information, information technology, and the presentation, analysis, evaluation, and citation of information. A bibliography, glossary, and index are included. This book is aimed at the college-level student and is useful to the inexperienced researcher.

CHAPTER SIX ▶▶▶▶▶▶▶▶ Periodicals and Indexes

Teaching students how to work with periodical information is a major part of any program for information literacy. Within the context of a formal course in information literacy, it is often the case that more time will be spent on periodical information—what a periodical is, what types of periodicals exist, how to identify periodical articles on a topic, how indexing and abstracting databases work, how to locate periodicals once a citation is found—than on any other single topic. Using periodicals as sources of information seems to be most preferred by students and is often required by their instructors. The exercises in this chapter provide a number of examples that have proved effective in exploring the multifaceted topic of periodical research, but, of course, there are many other similar exercises available, and even more yet to be created.

USING PERIODICALS

After becoming comfortable with using library catalogs to identify and locate books, students are now ready to face the more complicated task of researching their topic using periodical articles.

Before searching for articles in indexes and indexing and abstracting databases, it is helpful to establish clearly what a periodical is. The *International Encyclopedia of Information and Library Science* defines a periodical as "a publica-tion appearing at regular and fixed intervals of time under a distinctive title. . . . Its contents are usually some mixture of articles, reviews, stories or other writings by several contributors."[1] Periodicals can be published daily, weekly, monthly, quarterly, and so on.

It is helpful to remind students why periodicals are useful sources when doing research. Periodicals are important sources because they are published more frequently than books, they are more accessible, and they appear in a more finished form than other sources in the information cycle such as conference papers, patents, or working papers shared between colleagues. In general, periodicals tend to be the place where new knowledge is first revealed. Periodicals usually contain the most current information on a topic. Currency is especially important for science and social sciences research topics.

To really understand what periodicals are and how they differ from one another requires an even closer look, or an understanding of the taxonomy of periodicals. In our taxonomy, we divide periodicals into three major categories:

Popular magazines and newspapers

Professional, trade, and industry or special interest periodicals

Scholarly, academic, peer-reviewed, or refereed journals

The quality and characteristics of the information found in each type of periodical vary. The criteria below will help students understand the characteristics of each type and how to distinguish between them.

The material in figure 6-1 should be considered broad guidelines and should not be taken as absolute rules.

Look at the...	Popular magazines and newspapers	Professional, trade, and industry or special interest periodicals	Scholarly, academic, peer-reviewed, or refereed journals
Citation: *Title*	May have "magazine" or popular words in the title, e.g., *BusinessWoman, Mother Jones, People Weekly*	Sometimes has "news" in the title, e.g., *Metal Construction News, AAUP News.* Titles tend to be short and practical, e.g., *Beverage World* or *Hotel Business*	May have "journal," "bulletin," or "review" in the title, e.g., *Bulletin of Atomic Scientists, Journal of Soil and Water Conservation, International Review of Hydrobiology*
Citation: *Frequency of publication*	Issued frequently: weekly, biweekly, or monthly	Issued frequently: weekly, biweekly, or monthly	Issued less frequently: monthly, quarterly, or semiannually
Citation: *Authors of articles*	Often one author. Staff-written or written by freelance authors or guest contributors	Often one author. Staff-written or written by freelance authors, guest contributors, or professionals in the field	Frequently multiple co-authors. Scholars and researchers in the field, discipline, or specialty. Authors with university affiliations or professional titles
Citation: *Article length*	Articles usually short	Articles usually short	Longer articles (more than three pages)
Citation: *Article titles*	Popular or catchy article titles	Straightforward article titles, sometimes popular and catchy	Titles related to research question or results; often long, not catchy
Whole Periodical: *Paper, Illustrations, Layout*	Eye-catching covers, glossy paper, photos, illustrations, cartoons, sidebars	Eye-catching covers, glossy paper, photos, illustrations, cartoons, sidebars	Plain covers, usually plain matte paper; mostly text inside, with tables, figures, charts, graphs; little or no color or illustrations
Whole Periodical: *Advertising*	Many ads for general consumer products and services	Many ads for products and services related to a particular profession, trade, or industry	Few or no ads; if any, tend to be for other journals or specific services or products
Whole Periodical: *Tone*	Slick, glossy, attractive	Slick, glossy, attractive	Serious

FIGURE 6-1
Taxonomy of Periodicals

Look at the...	Popular magazines and newspapers	Professional, trade, and industry or special interest periodicals	Scholarly, academic, peer-reviewed, or refereed journals
Whole Periodical: *Audience*	Educated but non-expert readers; uses simple language in order to meet minimum education levels	Practitioners of a particular profession, members of a trade, or workers in an industry; language appropriate for an educated readership; assumes a certain level of specialized knowledge	Scholars and researchers in the field, discipline, or specialty; language contains terminology and jargon of the discipline; reader is assumed to have a scholarly background
Whole Periodical: *Purpose*	Designed to entertain or persuade readers with a variety of general interest topics in broad subject fields; also geared to sell products and services through advertising	Examines problems or concerns in a particular profession or industry; provides specialized information to a wide, interested audience	To inform, report, or make available original research or experimentation in a specific field or discipline to the rest of the scholarly world; where "new knowledge" is reported
Whole Periodical: *Availability*	Likely to be found on a newsstand or in a magazine store	Rarely found on a newsstand or in a magazine store; requires subscription or library access	With some exceptions, not found on a newsstand or in a magazine store; requires subscription or library access
Articles: *Abstracts*	Articles do not have an abstract at the beginning	Articles do not have an abstract at the beginning	Articles usually have an abstract at the beginning that summarizes the findings of the article
Articles: *References*	Sources are not cited; no references or bibliography at end of articles	Sources are not cited; no references or bibliography at end of articles	Scholarly references in the form of bibliographies, reference lists, and footnotes appear with each article
Examples:	*Glamour, People Weekly, Reader's Digest, Newsweek*	*Beverage World, Restaurant News, Advertising Age*	*Science, JAMA: Journal of the American Medical Association, Academy of Management Journal, Psychological Bulletin*

THE TAXONOMY OF PERIODICALS

Goal: In **exercise 26** students will familiarize themselves with different types of periodicals that they will encounter during their research. This exercise also reinforces the critical thinking emphasized throughout this book.

Description: Students will work in teams of two or three. The instructor will pass out the worksheet to each group along with three periodical titles, all related to the same general topic. One of the three should be from each category of periodical as defined on p. 59. Students will closely examine each periodical and decide which of the three categories it falls under and why. After students have completed the exercise, the groups will introduce their periodicals to the rest of the class, explaining the characteristics of each.

In figure 6-2 are some examples of groups of periodicals that have been used in this exercise.

Tips for conducting this exercise: You may wish to bring two copies of each of the three publications. This way, more than one student in each group can examine the same periodical at the same time. This in-class exercise can easily be adapted as a take-home assignment.

This exercise addresses ACRL Standard 1, Part 2, and Standard 3, Parts 2 and 6.

Popular magazine	Professional, trade, and industry or special interest periodical	Scholarly, academic, or research journal
Sports Illustrated	*Coach and Athletic Director*	*Research Quarterly for Exercise and Sport*
Business Week	*Adweek*	*Journal of Marketing Research*
Rolling Stone	*Billboard*	*American Music*
Prevention	*Drug Store News*	*Journal of the American Pharmaceutical Association*
American Gardener	*American Nurseryman*	*Journal of the American Society for Horticultural Science*

FIGURE 6-2
Examples of Periodical Groupings for Exercise 26

EXERCISE 26

The Taxonomy of Periodicals

Work in pairs or threes. Each group will be given three periodicals. Take a few minutes to look carefully at each periodical. *As a group*, discuss the characteristics of each. Using the criteria presented in the Taxonomy of Periodicals in figure 6-1 please decide in which category (popular magazine; professional, trade, and industry or special interest periodical; or scholarly, academic, or research journal) each of your periodicals best fits. Then, on a sheet of paper with your names at the top, write the titles of each of your periodicals, what type of periodical you think each is, and why you came to this conclusion, providing specific evidence from the periodicals themselves. Be prepared to introduce each of your periodicals to the class and to explain why it is a good representative of its category.

ACCESS TOOLS

Once students understand the different types of periodicals that exist and the unique characteristics of each, they are ready to learn how to use an access tool to systematically identify periodical articles about a topic.

Today's students are very familiar with the idea of typing words into a computer when using an Internet search engine or directory such as Google or Yahoo! and having search results magically appear before their eyes. We feel that students should be taken deeper into how access tools of any kind work. Instead of starting with on-line periodical indexes, which seem almost as magic as a web search, it helps to begin with the basics: Have students create a simple access tool to search for items in a collection.

CREATING AN ACCESS TOOL

Goal: In **exercise 27**, students will gain a basic foundation of what indexing is. After building their own access tool, periodical indexes will make more sense to them, both print indexes and on-line indexing and abstracting databases.

Description: Students will work in teams of two or three. The instructor will give each group an index card with an imaginary collection written on it. Students are to assume that their collection has twenty-five items. They will identify common characteristics of the items in the collection and select the three they feel are most important (for example, author, title, subject). These will become their access points. They will then list each item and the specific individual characteristics of each, which will enable them to perform a simple search of the collection.

Tips for conducting the exercise: This exercise can also be used individually as a take-home assignment, in which case the instructor may wish to suggest that students use a computer software program such as Microsoft Word, Microsoft Excel, or Microsoft Access to create the graphical representation of their collection.

Collections that have been used for this exercise include a collection of souvenirs; a collection of recipes; a collection of musical sound recordings; contact information for members of an organization, association, or team; the clothes in a closet; the items in a refrigerator.

This exercise addresses ACRL Standard 1, Part 2; Standard 2, Parts 2 and 5; and Standard 3, Parts 3 and 6.

PRINT INDEXES

Goal: In **exercise 28** students will gain an understanding of what an index is. Students will also gain appreciation of the time it takes to search print indexes and learn the difference between a general index and subject-specific indexes. Finally, they will learn that it is still sometimes necessary to use print indexes to gain access to older material.

Description: Students work with the *Readers' Guide to Periodical Literature* and two subject-specific indexes from H. W. Wilson. They complete a worksheet in class or at home that guides them through using these research tools.

Tips for conducting the exercise: If possible, make each student's worksheet slightly different (such as requiring an article from a different year) to avoid the entire class needing to work with the same print volume.

This exercise addresses ACRL Standard 1, Part 2.

GENERAL PERIODICALS DATABASES

After introducing students to print indexes, an appropriate next step is to show them the library's general periodicals database, for example ProQuest's Research Library, EBSCO's Academic Search Premier, or Gale's Expanded Academic Index.

We often use the exercise "Information and Time," found in chapter 3 of this book, to give students practice in using an on-line database. This exercise also serves to reinforce the taxonomy of periodicals.

To supplement any exercise, instructors can assign students the task of finding several articles in the general database on their research topic. This is similar to the assignment described in the introduction to subject-specific periodicals databases below.

EXERCISE 27

Creating an Access Tool

Carla J. List, a librarian and teacher of information research at Plattsburgh State University of New York (SUNY), writes in the second edition of her book *Information Research*, "A tool is something you use to help you accomplish a task. In the case of information research, an access tool is an information source that helps you by leading you to information. It may provide the actual material that you'll read or view, or it may only give you enough information to find that material."[2]

To create an access tool you must investigate the material in a collection and then explain, create, and devise systems you could use to organize the collection.

For this assignment, your team of two or three people will be given an index card with a type of collection written on it. You are to assume that there are twenty-five items in your collection, which you must organize (for example, recipes, music recordings, contact information for twenty-five people, and so on).

Make a list of the twenty-five specific items in your collection. Use your imagination!

Describe your collection by listing a number of important characteristics the items in the collection all have, such as age, size, shape, color, place of origin, cultural importance, genre or type, location, and so on.

Create a table listing each item in your collection and each item's three most important characteristics. Below is an example for a collection of jewelry with six items. On a separate sheet of paper, give an example of a search you could do in your collection, using two of your access points. For example, using the collection below, you could search for "expensive and ring." Which items would appear in your "results list"?

Jewelry Piece (item)	Value	Material	Type
Gold chain, 22k	Expensive	Gold	Necklace
Lorus watch	Cheap	Stainless steel	Watch
Swatch watch	Cheap	Plastic	Watch
Gold ring from India, 22k	Expensive	Gold	Ring
Silver bangle	Cheap	Sterling silver	Bracelet
Sapphire ring	Expensive	Sterling silver	Ring

EXERCISE 28

Print Indexes

In this exercise, you will be working with three periodical indexes in print format: the *Readers' Guide to Periodical Literature*, the *Humanities Index*, and the *Social Sciences Index*. These indexes are published by the H. W. Wilson Co., which has been producing them under one title or another since the early 1900s.

This worksheet will guide you through a few searches in these indexes. The goal of the exercise is to familiarize you with how print indexes work. This will also help you understand what goes on "behind the screen" when you search an on-line periodical database.

Using the *Readers' Guide to Periodical Literature*, find an article published in [year] having to do with school violence. Write the citation for the article.

Use the library's catalog to find out if this library has *this issue* of this periodical. Indicate below whether or not the library has the issue, and, if it does, write the information necessary to locate the article.

Is this article from a scholarly journal or a popular magazine?

Find an article published in [year] having to do with school violence using the *Social Sciences Index*. Write the citation for the article.

Which libraries in [name of your consortium] could supply this article? Name the libraries.

Is this article from a scholarly journal or a popular magazine?

_____

Find an article by N. Turner about the painter Paul Cézanne, using the *Humanities Index*. Write the citation for the article.

Is it possible to find this article in [name of your library]? Indicate where it would be located. Be specific.

Which of the indexes above is the best for finding articles published about market research?

What index would you use to find scholarly articles on philosophy?

In what index would you look to find a news article about Ronald Reagan being elected president of the United States in 1980?

CREATING DATABASE SEARCH STATEMENTS

After students have gotten their feet wet with the library's general-purpose on-line indexing and abstracting database, they will need practice turning their research question into a search statement that databases can understand. Many students will be used to tools on the World Wide Web, such as "Ask Jeeves," where they can type in a complete question and get acceptable search results. While some library databases are incorporating such "natural language" searches, it is still standard practice when searching indexing and abstracting databases to use Boolean logic. Being able to take a research question, identify its core concepts, think of alternate search terms, and structure a Boolean search from these elements is essential to students' research success. Without this skill, students will get poor results when they search library databases and their research will not be effective.

Goal: In **exercise 29** students will learn to create search statements that a database will understand.

Description: Students will work in teams of two or three. Each group will be given an index card with a research question on it. They will identify the key concepts in the question and brainstorm possible synonyms or alternate ways of phrasing each concept. Finally, they will create a Boolean search statement that will effectively find results that address their research question. The instructor will call on as many groups as possible to have them read their research question aloud and explain their process to the class. Meanwhile, the instructor will write their words and statement on the board, with the rest of the class giving input about other synonyms or ways to phrase the search.

Tips for conducting the exercise: It is helpful if the instructor begins the class with a refresher on the Boolean operators *and*, *or*, and *not*. A solid understanding of Boolean searching should be enough to enable students to create effective search statements on any topic.

This exercise can easily be followed up with an exercise in searching subject-specific databases. For example, students who created a search statement in the area of literature could run their search statement through the *MLA Bibliography*. This would give them familiarity with the database and also allow them to test the effectiveness of the search statement they created.

Here are three examples of research questions in the humanities, social sciences, and sciences that have been used for this exercise.

Humanities

Frederick Law Olmstead (1822–1903) was a landscape architect who designed a number of public parks, including Central Park in New York City. Olmstead was well-known for his political opinions; for example, he was a vocal opponent of slavery. He was also the founder of the *Nation*, the oldest continuously published American periodical in existence and still one of the leading liberal magazines of its kind. How were Olmstead's political views reflected in his designs of public space?

Social Sciences

There are many arguments for and against the legalization of illicit drugs. One argument for legalization states that overall demand for illegal drugs would go down if drugs were legalized because the allure of doing something forbidden would disappear. Find both support for and criticism of this viewpoint.

Science

With the ongoing destruction of rain forests and other habitats, the number of plant and animal species facing extinction continues to grow. What are the implications of this loss of biodiversity on the development of new pharmaceutical drugs?

This exercise addresses ACRL Standard 1, Part 1 and Standard 2, Parts 2, 3, and 4.

EXERCISE 29

Creating Effective Search Statements

Each group of two or three students will receive an index card with a research question on it. Working as a group, please:

   Pick out the key concepts in your research question.

   If appropriate, list some synonyms or alternate ways of phrasing each of your key concepts. Use the form below.

Key Concept	Synonyms or Alternate Ways of Phrasing

   Structure a search statement that you could use for researching this topic in a database. Use Boolean operators (*and, or, not*) when appropriate.

   Be prepared to share your research question, key concepts and synonyms, and search statement with the class.

SUBJECT-SPECIFIC PERIODICALS DATABASES

Described below is a major project on subject-specific indexing and abstracting databases. This Team Database Discovery Project is used in the context of a three-credit course in which it alone accounts for 10 percent of each student's grade.

There are many active learning methods by which students can become familiar with the many indexing and abstracting databases available in libraries. For example, an exercise similar to exercise 28 could be used to guide students step-by-step through a number of databases.

Alternately, students could be required to complete an assignment in which they search for six periodical articles on a semester research topic by using at least three subject-specific databases. They will submit printouts of the database records with subject terms circled; printouts of each periodical's bibliographic record from the on-line catalog; a photocopy or printout of the first page of each article found; a list of citations to each article in proper format followed by an analysis of why that article is or is not relevant to their topic; and finally, a comparison of the scope and the types of citations found in each database.

DATABASE DISCOVERY PROJECT

Goal: In **exercise 30** students will gain an in-depth understanding of one indexing and abstracting database and a familiarity with several more. Students will learn the basic characteristics and features of many of the databases they will be using throughout their academic careers. The common characteristics of all databases will emerge, further empowering students to learn on their own in the future.

Description: For this project, students work in teams of three or four to investigate a particular subject-specific indexing and abstracting database assigned by the instructor. The students are guided by a worksheet that asks specific questions. They have a certain amount of time to discover the database, after which they are expected to teach the database to the entire class in a presentation of ten to fifteen minutes. Students are encouraged to use visual aids such as posters and handouts to enhance the quality of their presentation. Each group is graded on a number of criteria by the other members of the class and by the instructor. Criteria include the group's effectiveness in presenting the overall description and scope of the database; examples of basic searches and features; examples of advanced searches and features; and proper determination of the audience for the database, that is, who would use it. Students' final grade on the project is a combination of the grades given by their peers and those given by the instructor.

Tips for conducting the exercise: Students should be given some time during one or more class meetings to work on this project. They will also need to get together outside of class to organize their presentation, come up with sample searches, design visual aids and handouts, and so forth—a fact that should be emphasized. This project is a fair amount of work, and the instructor's expectations should be made clear. Based on particular teaching situations, the amount of class time students can be given to discover their databases will vary, as will the time between starting the project and giving the class presentations.

This exercise addresses ACRL Standard 2, Part 1.

EXERCISE 30

Database Discovery Project

Three to four students will be assigned a specific database. The team will have [this class period] to discover the features of the database and learn how to use it. During our class meeting [date], each team will teach the rest of the class how to use their database. Each team's Database Discovery presentation will be evaluated by the team's classmates as well as the instructor. Your final grade will be a combination of these grades.

Each presentation should take approximately ten to fifteen minutes. Every team member is required to actively participate in their group's presentation. If you want to do well on this project, be prepared to meet with your team outside of class to prepare your presentation and any visual aids or handouts that you will be using. The Database Discovery worksheet below will guide you in your discovery and help you structure your presentation.

A successful presentation will:

> Include information on the database's content, design, time period covered, audience, search capabilities (basic and advanced), and retrieval options.

> Include demonstrations and discussion of each item listed above and completely address the questions on the Database Discovery worksheet below.

> Be flexible—you should be able to explain any unexpected search results or problems that might crop up during your presentation and recover from them if they occur.

> Include attractive and informative visual aids and handouts.

Suggestion: Find the *help* or *about* or *news* screens for the database. This is where you can find many of the answers to the following questions.

PART ONE: DATABASE DESCRIPTION

> What is the name of your database?

> What organization is responsible for providing access to the database? (This is often called the "database vendor.")

> What is the name of the software created by this vendor for searching the database? (This is like a brand name for the screen interface.)

> What organization is responsible for creating the database? Is this the same or different from the database vendor?

Hint: Often a database will be created by a professional association, for example the American Economic Association creates the database EconLit. EconLit is then offered to subscribers through different vendors, each with its own interface. So a library can subscribe to EconLit through the organization OCLC, which calls its search interface FirstSearch. Or it is possible to subscribe to EconLit through the company Cambridge Scientific Abstracts. This organization calls its search interface CSA Internet Database Service. Yet another vendor that carries EconLit is EBSCO Information Services, through their software named EBSCOhost.

> Find an overview or explanation of the database. Tell us what the database is all about.

> What subject areas or disciplines does the database cover?

(Continued)

Who do you think would be the most likely users of this database? Think of as many different groups as you can and list them in order of most likely to use. Explain your answer.

Try to find out how big the database is. How many entries, or records, does the database contain? What does this mean?

What types of materials are included as sources in the database? (Books, book chapters, journal articles, magazine articles, newspaper articles, conference proceedings, patents, web sites, government publications, and so on.)

How many different sources does the database index? Give an example of two or three titles.

What time period or years does the database cover? What does this mean?

Are the sources indexed in the database all English-language sources? If not, what other languages are included?

Does the database provide the full text or content of the articles it indexes? If so, does it provide the full text for *all* articles indexed?

If the database does not provide full text, then what does it give you? Explain and describe.

How often is the database updated (that is, how often are new records added)?

PART TWO: DATABASE USABILITY

Find the database's Help or User Guide screens. How do they work? What do they include? Is the help easy or difficult to understand? Do you think it is helpful? What is most helpful in the help section?

Does the database use a "controlled vocabulary?" (If you aren't sure what this is, take a look at your class notes or the glossary in the back of your textbook.) Is there a Subject Thesaurus or a Subject Terms list? Find out and be able to explain what it is and demonstrate how to use it. How easy is it to use?

How does one search this database?

Is it user-friendly or difficult to figure out?

By what access points does the database allow you to search?

Be able to demonstrate and describe several methods for searching the database.

Does the database offer advanced search mechanisms? Be able to demonstrate and describe any.

What fields are included in the full record for an item? Show us a record and identify the fields.

Does the database offer Boolean searching? Be able to demonstrate how to set up a Boolean search.

Explain all of the different ways that information from the database can be retrieved (for example, by marking records, reformatting records, printing records, e-mailing records, and saving records to disk).

In preparation for your presentation, be sure to take clear and comprehensive notes while you are in database discovery mode. For example, write down the path to any help screens you might want to show the class. Note any searches you did that would be especially useful in demonstrating the database's features.

This chapter has provided an overview of the universe of information student researchers will encounter in periodical publications and of the tools researchers use to identify information relevant to their needs within this ever-expanding universe.

One aspect of this search for periodical information that was not emphasized was how to actually find the articles identified. Therefore, if possible, supplement the exercises presented in this chapter with a full discussion of how to physically locate the information identified, including using the library catalog to determine if the library (or other libraries in a consortium) owns the periodical and, if so, where it is shelved. Include alternatives for obtaining the article, such as interlibrary loan or visiting other local libraries.

NOTES

1. John Feather and Paul Sturges, eds., *International Encyclopedia of Information and Library Science* (London: Routledge, 1997).
2. Carla J. List. *Information Research*, 2nd ed. (Dubuque, Iowa: Kendall/Hunt, 2002), p. 40.

CHAPTER SEVEN

The Web and Scholarly Research

While many of today's students spend a great deal of time surfing the Web and consider themselves savvy web searchers, others have had very little experience with it. Not surprisingly, differences in students' levels of experience often fall along the lines of economic background, race, and age. For this reason, when teaching the Web as a research tool, it is important to start with the basics. What exactly *is* the Internet? What is the history of the Internet? Who can put information up on the Web, and how? And what is the World Wide Web specifically, in comparison to the Internet as a whole? Just a brief outline of the technology of the Internet in the simplest terms will benefit all students, not only those who are inexperienced.

In the context of information literacy, it is of great importance to go into some detail about where the information on the Web comes from. Who creates it? What kind of organizations and individuals publish information to the World Wide Web? Who is their intended audience? What is their purpose? How is their purpose likely to affect the information they provide?

Just as students learned to differentiate between general, trade, and scholarly periodicals, they should understand the difference between the types and orientation of information found on the sites of government agencies (.gov) such as the Census Bureau or the Bureau of Justice Statistics; educational institutions (.edu) such as universities and some research institutions and museums such as the Smithsonian Institute; organizations or associations (.org), including issue-based organizations like the American Civil Liberties Union or the NAACP; and industry and professional associations like the Toy Industry Association or the American Medical Association. In addition, there is what is now the largest category of web sites, commercial sites (.com) that exist to advertise or sell a product or service.

Many students use web sites as information sources for high school and college assignments. In fact, search engines such as Google are often the first place they turn when faced with a research project. They often seem unaware of the rich variety and depth of information resources available through their school, college or university, and public libraries that are simply unavailable on the Web. Librarians hear directly from teachers and professors that they are unhappy with the quality of information students are using, or they hear through the students that their instructors have arbitrarily ruled that they are "not allowed to use any information from the Internet."

This again stresses the importance, emphasized throughout these chapters, that students must learn to critically evaluate the quality of the information they find so that they can make intelligent decisions about whether or not it is appropriate for academic use. Nowhere is this more true than for information they find on the Web.

SEARCHING THE WORLD WIDE WEB

After a general introduction to the Internet, students should learn about searching the Web in some depth, just as they learned what goes on "behind the screen" of indexing and abstracting databases in chapter 6. Most students know how to go to Yahoo!, Google, Ask Jeeves, or any number of sites for searching the Internet and type in a few words related to what they want to find. They need to learn that each of these Internet search tools has its own strengths and weaknesses, methods of indexing, and advanced search capabilities.

Students should learn some of the specifics of these sites for searching the Web. For example, web directories are organized by people who select the sites to be included, and web search engines are compiled by computer programs known as "spiders" or "crawlers" that crawl through the Web, indexing sites according to preprogrammed algorithms. Some search engines index the words in the title of the web page only, while some index the title and the lead paragraphs, and others the entire page. The databases of different search engines are refreshed periodically, and the frequency that they are refreshed will affect search results. The relative size of the major search engines and directories varies widely. Search engines rank web pages based on different criteria. An excellent source of this kind of information for instructors and students is the web site Search Engine Watch.[1]

Web directories and search engines, like library databases, have help screens that will explain how to search most effectively. These screens will outline the search syntax of the site and any advanced search features. For example: Is Boolean searching supported? How do you search for a phrase? Does the search engine assume that there is an *and* between your search terms? Will the search *Italian recipes* find information on the concept "Italian recipes," or will it find pages with either word anywhere in the page? Does it matter if you type *Italian* or *italian*? Can you limit your search, for example, to have the search engine only show results from the .gov domain?

Specialty search engines are available, for example those designed to find results in a particular subject area, such as law or health, and multi-media search engines that allow one to search only for sound, image, or video files. There are also search engines called "metacrawlers," which allow a search to be sent to several search engines at once with the results appearing on one page.

These are but some of the many factors that will affect the outcome of students' Web searches. Searchers' understanding of how to structure a search according to the characteristics of the particular search tool will allow them more control over the search and will produce better results.

"SHOULD I USE A LIBRARY DATABASE OR SHOULD I JUST SEARCH THE WEB?"

Goal: In **exercise 31** students will experience the differences between information found in periodical articles accessed through the library's general indexing and abstracting database, and the information found through searching the Web using a directory or search engine. The instructor can take this opportunity to prove to students that in most cases, a library database will yield more information-rich results with less time and effort than conducting the same search on the Web. A second goal is to familiarize students with Web search tools.

Description: Students work in teams of two or three people. Each team receives an index card containing a specific topic and related questions. Two teams in the room receive the same topic. Students follow the worksheet below to search for the answer to their questions, using the library's general periodicals database, a web directory, and a search engine. Then, of the sources they find, each team will identify the one that they believe best answers their questions while also being the most reputable source, and they will decide whether they would use that source for a college-level research assignment. Each team will share their source with the rest of the class, which will decide which of the sources found by each team on the same topic is better and why.

Tips for conducting the exercise: Select topics for which it will be relatively easy to find information in both a general periodicals database and on the Web. Picking topics that might be more likely to have "far-out" information on the Web, such as "extraterrestrials," can highlight the difference between information found in a library periodical database and on the Internet. Here are some examples of topics that have been used for this exercise:

Drug testing in the workplace (How common is it? Are there any problems with this practice?)

Breast cancer (What are the available treatments? Are there any new treatments on the horizon? If so, which are most promising?)

Extraterrestrials (How likely is it that intelligent life exists somewhere in the universe besides the planet Earth? What do scientists think about this issue?)

This exercise addresses ACRL Standard 1, Parts 1, 2, and 4; Standard 2, Parts 2 and 3; Standard 3, Parts 2, 4, and 6; and Standard 5, Part 1.

STRATEGIES FOR SEARCHING THE INTERNET

In preparation for the next exercise in this chapter, and as a logical follow-up to the randomness of the search results students may have encountered in the last exercise, it is a good idea to present students with a set of general strategies that will help them find information on the Web.

WHO WOULD KNOW?

Before beginning a search, researchers should consider where the information they are looking for would most likely be found. Who would be an authoritative source on the topic? For example, if the researchers want to know the weather in Chicago, they could go to Yahoo! and search for "weather and Chicago," but they might have to wade through a large number of irrelevant and unhelpful results. On the other hand, if the researchers directly consulted the Weather Channel site at http://weather.com/, it would take only seconds to find out the weather for the windy city. Likewise, if students wanted to know how many murders were committed in the United States last year, they could enter "murders and United States and [year]" into Alta Vista and face a long list of results. Or, the researchers could first

ask a librarian or think about who collects crime statistics nationwide. Searching Alta Vista for the "Bureau of Justice Statistics" will quickly lead to that site, which has the desired information.

USE SEARCHING SKILLS

Earlier chapters presented exercises for teaching students how to break down a research question into key concepts, come up with a list of possible synonyms for each potential search term, and then formulate a search statement that would be understood by library indexing and abstracting databases. Students should be reminded of these skills they have already acquired and be informed that such skills can also be applied to searching the Internet.

KNOW YOUR WEB SEARCH TOOL

For the best search results, students should know the basic characteristics of their Web search tool and how to most effectively enter their search, given the requirements of that site.

REMEMBER WHAT IS NOT AVAILABLE ON THE INTERNET

The Internet contains a wealth of information, some of it high quality from reputable sources and some of it low quality from questionable sources. However, we owe it to students to make them truly understand that there is a great deal of information that they will *not* find on-line. In fact, a study published in the journal *Nature* in 1999 found that even the most comprehensive search engine at that time was aware of no more than 16 percent of publicly accessible Web pages.[2] Furthermore, much has been written about the "Invisible Web," or "Deep Web," which contains information that cannot be indexed by search engines because it is hidden within databases.

Search tools such as library indexing and abstracting services are not available on the Web to just anyone; institutions or individuals must subscribe to them to gain access. In general, students should be aware that any proprietary or copyrighted information is not generally available

EXERCISE 31

Should I Use a Library Database or
Should I Just Search the Web?

For this exercise, you will work in teams of two or three. Each team will receive an index card containing a specific topic and related questions. One other team in the classroom will receive the same topic as your team. You will be competing with them to see which of you can find the highest quality, most reliable sources that answer or address your questions.

Look up your topic in the web search tool or library database indicated below and describe the results of your searches as prompted. As you note how each search tool or database responds to your query, don't forget to actually find the answer to your question, noting sources (either articles or web sites) that have the information you need. When you are finished, you will select one source from those you found that best answers your question and appears to be a high-quality, reputable source.

Be prepared to share your favorite source and how you found it with the class. Would you use this source for a college-level research assignment?

Web search tool or reference database	How did you enter your search? [be exact]	No. of hits	How are your results organized? (e.g., chronologically, by relevance, etc.)	What types of materials did you find? (e.g., web pages, periodical articles, studies; from which domain type, etc.)
Yahoo! http://www.yahoo.com/				
Alta Vista http://www.altavista.com/				
[Library's general periodical database]				

THE BEST SOURCES FOUND

URL (web addresses) or path [You may wish to bookmark the sites and articles you find, since you will need to get back to your favorites to show the class.]	Description of information found and who wrote it.

on-line for free, at least not legally. A good rule of thumb is that if an information resource costs money in print format, it probably costs money on the Web too, if it is also available there.

A huge amount of information is simply not available via the Internet, for free *or* for a fee. For example, "only about 8 percent of all journals are on the Web, and an even smaller fraction of books."[3] This is especially the case with older information. Some of the classics of world literature have been made available on scholarly web sites such as Project Gutenberg,[4] but those are but a tiny fraction of the written works of humankind, most of which sit in obscurity on the shelves of libraries and rare book rooms worldwide. In addition, the explosion of electronic information over the past few decades means that there are electronic archives, research datasets, and personal and organizational records "out there" that may never be preserved, not to mention made public.

The significance of all of this to researchers is that while the Internet can be an excellent place to conduct research, relying on it exclusively will mean missing a great deal of valuable information.

INFORMATION ON THE WEB

There is no place where evaluation is more relevant than in examining information found on the Web. This is because *anyone* can create a web site. Most web pages do not undergo any sort of editorial review process, as do books and periodical articles. Therefore, critical thinking skills and an active, questioning mind are needed to evaluate any information found on the Internet.

Criteria for Evaluating Web Information

Purpose of the site and intended audience

- Are the goals of the author stated? Is there a statement of scope, target audience, or purpose?
- Who is the site designed for? What audience is the site's author trying to reach?
- Is the site scholarly or popular?
- Does the site contain advertising? What might this tell you?

- What is the overall purpose of the site? To inform? Persuade or advocate? Entertain? Sell a product?

Authority and credibility of author

- Can the author of the site be identified? Is it clear who has ultimate responsibility for the content of the material, whether it be an individual or an organization?
- Is contact information given so that you can get in touch with the author or organization for clarification or more information?
- What are the author's qualifications? Does he or she list his or her occupation, years of experience, position, or education?
- Do you think the author has expertise on the subject?
- What is the author's institutional affiliation, if any? Is the author affiliated with an educational institution? A nonprofit organization? A company?
- What is the domain of the site (.edu, .gov, .org, .com)? Is it a commercial, governmental, organizational, academic, or personal site? From what country does it originate?
- Is this site connected to an organization of any sort? If so, what is the mission of this organization?

Accuracy and reliability of the information on the site

- Does the site appear to be well-researched?
- Are there references to sources of information supporting any statements made or viewpoints held?
- Is statistical information labeled clearly and easy to read?
- Are the sources for any factual or statistical information documented so that it can be verified in another source?
- What method of data collection or research was used by the author (if applicable)?
- Does the site include grammatical, spelling, or typographical errors?
- How does the site compare to print information resources available on this topic?

- If links to other sites are listed, are they quality sites?

Currency and timeliness of the information on the site

- When was this information published? Does the page list the date it was created?
- Does the page indicate when it was last updated?
- Are there any "dead" links—links to other sites that no longer work?

Objectivity or bias of the site

- Are the goals of the author clearly stated? Is there a statement of scope, target audience, or purpose?
- Does the site present many opinions on the topic or only one?
- Can you tell if the site contains mostly opinions or facts?
- Can you identify any bias in the information and opinions provided?
- Is the site sponsored by a company or organization?
- Does the site reflect the agenda of a political, religious, or social group or institution?
- If there is advertising on the site, is it clearly differentiated from the informational content?

Structure and navigation of the site

- Is the organization of the site easy to understand? Is it clear and logical?
- Is it easy to navigate between different parts of the site?
- Is there a link to return to the first page of the site, the home page?
- Does the site offer a table of contents or a site index?
- Does the site offer a search box?
- Do graphics on the site add to or detract from the document itself?

Conclusion

- Is this site a reliable, well-documented source of information from a reputable author or organization?
- Would this be a good source of information for a research paper?

EVALUATING INFORMATION ON THE WEB

Goal: In **exercise 32** students will also be made aware that there is some very highly questionable information on the Internet that often masquerades as legitimate. They will learn to identify quality information and spot the differences between "good" and "bad" information.

Description: The instructor selects pairs of web sites related to the same topic. One site is legitimate: It is a reputable site that could be used as a quality source for a research project. The other site is of questionable quality. Students are divided into teams of two for this exercise. Each team gets one web site, so that two teams are working on the same topic. One team has the reputable site and another has the site of questionable quality. Students spend twenty or thirty minutes evaluating their sites, using the Criteria for Evaluating Web Information above. Then each team shows its site to the rest of the class and explains their evaluation of the site, pointing to evidence on the site that supports their view.

Tips for conducting the exercise: Topics and sites that have been used for this exercise include:

Martin Luther King Jr.

Martin Luther King Jr.: A Historical Examination
http://www.martinlutherking.org/

The Martin Luther King Jr. Papers Project
http://www.stanford.edu/group/King/index.htm

UFOs

CAUS: Citizens Against UFO Secrecy
http://caus.org/

SETI Institute
http://www.seti-inst.edu/

Greenhouse Effect

CO2 and Climate Resource Center
http://www.greeningearthsociety.org/

EPA Global Warming Site
http://yosemite.epa.gov/oar/globalwarming.
nsf/content/index.html

Many sites created by librarians have lists of web sites that are very good for this type of assignment.[5]

This exercise addresses ACRL Standard 1, Parts 1, 2, and 4; Standard 2, Part 2; Standard 3, Parts 2, 4, 5, and 6; and Standard 5, Part 1.

EXERCISE 32

Evaluating Information on the Web

For this exercise, you will work in teams of two. Each team will receive an index card with the address of a web site on it. You will have approximately twenty to thirty minutes to complete this exercise.

Go to the web site and explore it thoroughly, then evaluate the site using the Criteria for Evaluating Web Information just discussed. On a piece of paper, note the title and URL of your site and summarize your conclusions about the site's quality, noting specific evidence that supports your evaluation. Please be prepared to share your site and your evaluation of it with the class.

NOTES

1. Search Engine Watch, Jupitermedia Corporation, 1996-2002. Available at http://www.searchenginewatch.com/. Accessed 20 December 2002.
2. Steve Lawrence and C. Lee Giles, "Accessibility of information on the Web," *Nature* 400, no. 6740 (July 8, 1999): 107-9.
3. Mark Y. Herring, "Ten reasons why the Internet is no substitute for a library," *American Libraries* 32, no. 4 (April 2001): 76-78.
4. Project Gutenberg Official Home Site, Project Gutenberg and PROMO.NET, 1971-2002. Available at http://gutenberg.net/. Accessed 20 December 2002.
5. There are a number of sites created by librarians with links to web sites of questionable quality, created for the purposes of instructing students about the pitfalls of web research. A few of these are:

   Jan Alexander and Marsha Ann Tate, Evaluating web pages: Links to examples of various concepts. Available at http://www2.widener.edu/Wolfgram-Memorial-Library/webevaluation/examples.htm. Accessed 20 December 2002.

   Susan E. Beck, The good, the bad and the ugly: Or, why it's a good idea to evaluate web sources. Available at http://lib.nmsu.edu/instruction/evalexpl.html. Accessed 20 December 2002.

CHAPTER EIGHT ▶▶▶▶▶▶▶▶ Other Tools for Research

When students receive a research assignment, they tend to use resources they already know: reference books, journal articles, and web sites. They are frequently familiar with some or all of these sources and know that there is someone in the library who can help them locate and use other sources of information of the same kind.

EXPERTS AND ORGANIZATIONS

What does not come to mind so easily are human sources of information. There is a wealth of human knowledge and expertise on every college campus, in organizations throughout the world, and in local communities. For almost any topic imaginable, there exists a professional, trade, or special interest organization.

An example of a professional organization is the American Medical Association, whose members are doctors. The AMA provides professional information and networking opportunities to its members, educates the public and policy makers about health issues, and advocates for the interests of the medical community.

An example of a trade organization is the National Restaurant Association. This group is made up of individual restaurant owners and restaurant chains. Their goal is to represent, educate, and promote the restaurant industry and to advocate for governmental policies favorable to the industry.

An example of a special interest organization is the Surfrider Foundation, which is a nonprofit organization dedicated to protecting our oceans, waves, and beaches. Other examples of special interest organizations are the National Organization for Women, the NAACP, the American Civil Libraries Union, and Greenpeace.

IDENTIFICATION OF EXPERTS AND ORGANIZATIONS

How do students identify an appropriate expert or association? One method of identifying experts is to use a reference directory such as the *Encyclopedia of Associations*. This encyclopedia is indexed by the title and keyword for each organization. Entries show contact information and the scope of the organizations' activities. It is helpful to note that not all associations make information freely available to the public. Many limit information to members only.

Goal: In **exercise 33** students will learn to identify experts and organizations that can provide information about a specific topic.

Description: For this exercise, have students use a directory of associations in paper format or on-line. Students will identify individuals and organizations appropriate to their paper trail topic or to the instructor's assigned topic. The exercise may simply familiarize students with this type of directory or may instruct students to contact their chosen organizations and ask for information to be sent to them.

Tips for conducting the exercise: We have used the *Encyclopedia of Associations* and its online counterpart, Associations Unlimited. Any similar directory will work.

This exercise addresses ACRL Standard 2, Parts 1, 2, and 3.

EXERCISE 33

Finding Experts and Organizations

For this assignment you may use either the print copy of the *Encyclopedia of Associations* or the web version, which can be found on the Library Web Resources list under the title Associations Unlimited.

Look through the listings and select three for experts or associations most closely related to your topic. Report the information in the format requested below, giving specific information for each expert or organization.

Name of Organization: _____

Contact Information: _____

Description of What the Organization Does (scope) _____

_____

_____

_____

_____

_____

Web Address: _____

Now go to the web site for each expert or association. Is there any relevant information there? Print it out and attach it to this worksheet or describe it on the back of this page.

Contact one expert or association, using phone, mail, e-mail, or fax and ask them to send you information on your topic. Or create a list of short questions you'd like your expert or association to address. Attach the contact information and the list of questions (if relevant) to the response you receive and submit.

Statistics

Another type of information that can be useful in research is statistics. Statistics are facts and data. Statistics is also the science that deals with collection, classification, analysis, and interpretation of facts and or data. Our world is filled with statistics. Every individual in the United States is counted in the census, has a Social Security number, lives in a ZIP code area, has an account of one sort or another, goes to school, has a flu shot, registers a car, or becomes a statistic in some other way. The U.S. government is the largest compiler of statistical information in the world. Many other groups and individuals collect statistics as well.

Types of Statistics

Descriptive statistics use numbers to summarize the information collected concerning a particular situation. For example: A random sample of students was taken at a university campus in Providence, Rhode Island. Of those questioned, 15 percent used Five Star notebooks for their course note-taking. This descriptive statistic is a kind of shorthand for what actually happened. One hundred forty students at the university campus in Providence, Rhode Island, were asked what kind of notebook they used for notetaking. Twenty-one of those students used Five Star notebooks. Doing the math required to change these numbers into a percentage resulted in the descriptive statistic above.

Statistical inference is the use of numbers to make generalizations or predictions about what a large group of people will do based on what a smaller group of people did. For example: Using the raw data above (of 140 Rhode Island students, 21 use Five Star notebooks = 15 percent use Five Star notebooks), statistical inference might claim that on the basis of the information collected that 15 percent of all university students in New England capital cities use Five Star notebooks.

This statistic implies that students in New England capital cities use Five Star notebooks, even though students in only one New England capital city were questioned. Statistical inference might use the Providence statistic to infer some-thing about a larger population. Claims made through statistical inference must be examined very carefully for accuracy and probability. There may be forces at work in Providence causing university students there to buy Five Star notebooks that do not extend to all New England cities. To infer that what happens in Providence happens elsewhere in New England may be inaccurate or even incorrect. The sample size for the study of notebook use was fairly small—only 140 students were questioned. It might be that those students all live in the vicinity of the same mall that carries Five Star notebooks. Or perhaps the students surveyed were all contacted at the same time of day. Those students taking day classes might have different options for purchasing Five Star notebooks than those who attend classes at night. A survey of a larger number of people over a longer period of time might give very different results, which would then change what could be inferred from the statistic collected.

WHERE DO STATISTICS COME FROM?

The U.S. government is the largest collector and compiler of statistics in the world. Government agencies collect their own statistics. For example, the Census Bureau, the Bureau of Economic Analysis, the Bureau of Labor Statistics, the National Center for Education Statistics, the Bureau of Justice Statistics, the National Center for Health Statistics, and the Bureau of Transportation Statistics are all government agencies specializing in the collection of statistics.

In the international community, there are intergovernmental organizations that collect data as well. For example, the United Nations, the World Bank/International Monetary Fund, and the OECD (Organization for Economic Cooperation and Development) are all intergovernmental agencies cooperating to collect data on a global scale.

Professional, trade, and special interest organizations also collect statistics. The American Library Association, the American Medical Association, the American Marketing Association, the American Bar Association, the Beer Institute, Amnesty International, Greenpeace, and the Toy Industry Association all are organizations that collect statistics.

There are also agencies, researchers, and individuals that collect statistics for various purposes. These groups or individuals tend to focus on specific topics such as attitudes of high school students toward drug use, whether the death penalty should be abolished, how popular the president of the United States is, or what the most-watched shows on television are. Much research and data collection is done at universities or research institutes or by opinion research firms. Results are reported in scholarly publications like journals and, in some cases, in the public media.

Strategies for Finding Statistical Information

When looking for statistical information, it is important to look for some key facts. The first question to ask is, Who would collect this information? For example, if we were looking for statistics on how many people were put to death in the United States last year under the death penalty laws, it would be necessary to consider what organization or department of the government might gather and publish that statistic. The death penalty is administered at the state level, so it might be possible to check every state, but perhaps there is one place where the information is compiled. The federal government is likely to collect and compile the statistics from the states concerning the number of people put to death under the death penalty laws. What part of the federal government might do this? The department in charge of law enforcement might be a good place to start, so the Department of Justice is the logical place. This department has a Bureau of Justice Statistics. While an individual may not know of the existence of this bureau, by following a logical thought process and looking for the existence of such a department or division, it should not be too difficult to find the name of an appropriate agency. Many U.S. government agencies and departments have web sites, and they are all listed in various government manuals.

Another possibility for finding this statistic would be to identify an organization either in support of or in opposition to the death penalty. These organizations would be sure to have the statistic, although it might be important to watch for possible manipulation in how they report or use that statistic. In fact, it might be a good idea to get the same statistic from more than one source to ensure the reliability of the number. Organizations in favor of or against a certain cause are likely to be listed in the *Encyclopedia of Associations*.

Finally, it might be possible to find up-to-date statistics in a newspaper or magazine article about the death penalty. Newspaper indexes are available in most libraries in paper, microform, or online formats.

USING STATISTICAL SOURCES

Goal: **Exercise 34** will familiarize students with sources of statistical information.

Description: In this exercise students will use selected sources of statistical information to answer specific questions. They will achieve some practice in looking for, accessing, and retrieving statistical information. This exercise can be done in class or as a homework assignment.

Tips for conducting the exercise: The sections can be broken into smaller assignments, depending on your need and time available. Check the web sites before handing out the assignment to make sure that they are still correct and active.

This exercise addresses ACRL Standard 2, Parts 3, 4, and 5.

EXERCISE 34

Using Statistical Sources

Using the Toy Industry Association web site, answer the following questions. The TIA web site can be found at: www.toy-tia.org. Click on Industry. Then click on Statistics.

What two retailers sell the greatest percentage of toys?

How much money did the toy industry spend in 1999 on advertisements shown on cable TV?

What was the total value in 1999 of shipments of action figure toys? (Watch your decimal places.)

What was the value in 1999 of shipments of doll houses and furniture? (Watch your decimal places.)

Did the United States import or export more toys in 1999?

Access the Kids Count web site at: www.aecf.org/kidscount/ to answer the following questions. From this address, click on Kids Count Databook Online.

How many children are there in the United States under the age of 18?

How many high school drop-outs were counted for the most current year in the United States?

What state had the highest percentage of high school drop-outs in the latest year reported?

Create a line graph for the percentage of families with children headed by a single parent. Select Connecticut, Massachusetts, and Rhode Island as your geographic region. Select the time period that covers the most current 5 years. Print your graph and attach. Which state has the highest percentage of single-parent households?

Create a map for infant mortality rates for 1999. Name three states with a ranking more than 20 percent better than the median for all states.

Tools for Finding Statistics

One of the best places to start when you're looking for statistics is the *Statistical Abstract of the United States*, published annually since 1879 by the U.S. government. The *Statistical Abstract* presents statistics on many different topics from many different sources.

The *Statistical Abstract* can also lead you to other statistics sources. At the bottom of each statistical table in the *Statistical Abstract*, you will find a reference to the original sources of these statistics. By consulting the original source, you may find additional statistical information on that topic. For example, the *Statistical Abstract* has statistics on the number of CDs teenagers buy. At the bottom of the table containing those statistics, the Recording Industry Association of America, Inc., is listed as the source for the numbers. By going to the Recording Industry Association of America, Inc., web site, or by contacting them, it is likely that one could find additional statistics about the same topic. At the end of each edition of the *Statistical Abstract of the United States*, all the sources used for the statistical tables are listed. Keep in mind that each state has its own statistical abstract as well. The web sites and addresses are listed in this section of the *Statistical Abstract of the United States*.

USING THE *STATISTICAL ABSTRACT OF THE UNITED STATES*

Goal: **Exercise 35** will familiarize students with the *Statistical Abstract of the United States* and the wide variety of statistics that are collected each year. It will also help them identify other sources of statistics that the government uses.

Description: For this exercise, students should use the most current year of the *Statistical Abstract of the United States*. Using the paper version seems to be more useful for new users of this tool, but doing so can be difficult, as most libraries only have one or two copies available. The web version is more cumbersome to use, but it will serve more students at the same time.

Tips for conducting the research: Students may need some practice in using the electronic version, as it is a little more complicated than the paper.

This exercise addresses ACRL Standard 2, Parts 3, 4, and 5.

EVALUATING STATISTICAL INFORMATION

Being able to evaluate statistical information is important, as statistics can be manipulated to tell the story that the person using them wants to tell. We have all heard how it is possible to lie with statistics. However, evaluating statistical information can be a very difficult task, and in some cases is something that only experts or others with advanced knowledge of statistics know how to do. It requires an in-depth understanding of the data-gathering process and the mathematical techniques used to generate the statistics.

However, with some common sense, everyone can learn to be wary and critical of the numbers they find and can avoid being duped by statistics. Here are a few general points to keep in mind when working with statistical information.

Who collected the data? Do they have a particular interest in the results?

Do the statistics show any bias?

Are the data timely?

Is the coverage complete? What was the size of the sample for the study?

Has the data been repackaged?

Is the data from a primary source? If it is from a secondary source, has it been properly documented so that you can find the primary source?

Experts and organizations are frequently overlooked as sources of information. With the appropriate tools to identify the experts and the information that will allow students to contact those experts, a rich new field of possibilities for insight and information becomes available.

Statistics are part of our lives. Knowing how to find appropriate statistics can add a dimension to any research endeavor. With a little practice, a student can easily see that statistics can be collected and interpreted to show just about anything. Learning how to assess and evaluate a statistic and its veracity will serve students for the rest of their lives.

EXERCISE 35

Finding U.S. Government-Supplied Statistics

Using the *Statistical Abstract of the United States,* answer the following questions. List the table number where you found your answer.

It is a well-known fact within the music industry that the category of consumers spending the most money on CDs and tapes is teenagers. What percentage of all buyers of sound recordings are between the ages of 15 and 19?

How many deaths in the United States were caused by major cardiovascular disease?

How many travelers from the United States visited South America during the latest year reported?

How many overseas travelers visited California in the latest year reported?

How many existing one-family houses were sold in the United States and what was the median sales price?

What percentage of public schools have Internet access?

How much asparagus is commercially produced in the United States? What state is the leading producer ?

How much asparagus is used per capita (per person) in the United States?

CHAPTER NINE ▶▶▶▶▶▶▶▶▶ The Paper Trail Project

The quest of many of today's students is to do their research *fast*! Very often this involves good intentions, the Internet, and frequently some cut-and-paste. These efforts do not always produce the results intended by the student and are generally unacceptable to the instructor or professor on the receiving end of the assignment. Information literacy projects, courses, and programs can help to alleviate this frustration by teaching students the best and most efficient tools and techniques for using them.

At the University of Rhode Island, instructors use the semester-long Paper Trail Project as a vehicle for students to learn and apply information concepts and skills. These concepts and skills are experienced, practiced, learned, and applied by students in a number of smaller projects that culminate in the completion of the Paper Trail Project. This chapter will explain the goals of the project, the six major parts of the project as they are explained to students, and our rationale for including each part in the project. We will also identify how each of the ACRL Information Literacy Competency Standards applies to each part of the Paper Trail Project. A sample Paper Trail Project and a Student Time Line for completing the project conclude the chapter.

GOALS OF THE PAPER TRAIL PROJECT

The overall goal of the Paper Trail Project is for students to explore the information world by learning to use effective methods and techniques of information gathering, evaluation, and presentation. The knowledge gained from this project will prepare students to conduct university-level research and to develop skills necessary for lifelong learning. The project requires students to learn and show expertise in all of the ACRL Information Literacy Competency Standards. By participating in the Paper Trail Project, students will recognize that:

Research reflects real life because it *is* real life;

They *can* do quality research;

The research process continues throughout our lives in what is called "lifelong learning."

Simply described, the Paper Trail Project is an annotated, chronological "map" that follows the research journey for a research question of the student's design. Once completed, the six parts of the project will accomplish the student goals and the objectives of the Paper Trail Project. It should be noted that for this project the goal is to complete the research process and document it. It is not necessary for students to actually write the research paper itself.

SIX MAJOR PARTS OF THE PAPER TRAIL PROJECT

Introductory Research: Encyclopedia article, concept map, final research question, and an outline of the topic with major headings and enough subheadings to explain what it is you plan to research and how.   *(15 points)*

Research Journal: Journal of personal entries explaining the process (the steps you took to do the work) of the research, both successful and unsuccessful, and your personal experience with the research process.   *(20 points)*

Annotated Bibliography of Sources Used: A word-processed annotated bibliography of *twenty* high-quality, appropriate sources on your topic. Each annotation should include a brief summary of the item and an explanation of why you chose to include it in the project. This bibliography must include books, periodical articles, experts, and web sites.   *(20 points)*

Annotated Bibliography of Sources Not Used: A word-processed annotated bibliography of ten to twenty sources you decided not to use, with an evaluative explanation of why you decided not to use them.   *(20 points)*

Physical Proof of Searches: Printouts and photocopies of the results of your searches in library catalogs, periodical databases, and web search engines and directories. Printouts and photocopies of the title pages of the books, articles, web sites, and other information used. These will match the items in the annotated bibliographies.   *(15 points)*

Physical Results of Miscellaneous Sources: Items you have gathered that will support your research question and help to explain your research process. These may be from agencies, associations, organizations, institutions, or individual experts who are evaluated as appropriate for your research area. Materials may include such items as pamphlets, brochures, newsletters, personal letters, and documented interviews and other miscellaneous items.   *(10 points)*

(100 points total)

Explaining the Parts of the Paper Trail

PART 1: THE INTRODUCTORY RESEARCH AND PLANNING

This piece addresses ACRL Standard 1.

The students must ask themselves these questions: What is my question, problem, or thesis? How much information do I need? How big a question will I attempt to answer? How will I narrow or broaden the research?

The introductory research phase asks students to identify a topic of interest to them. This topic must be academic in nature and could be a topic being used for a project or semester paper in another class. If the student chooses a topic that seems more popular than academic, such as skateboarding, the instructor should steer the student to approach that topic from an academic point of view. For instance, "What is the physics and engineering history of skateboards?"

Refocusing and refining a research topic idea can be achieved through the brainstorming process of concept mapping. Once the student has developed an academic research topic, the student selects the subtopic ideas of greatest interest. From these subtopics the student develops a formal research question.

As a final step in completing Part 1, we ask the student to propose a basic outline for the possible research paper or project.

PART 2: THE RESEARCH JOURNAL

This piece addresses ACRL Standards 1 and 3.

The research journal provides a means for students to share personal, informal, self-revealing reflection and comments on the total research process. Some students are more comfortable than others sharing thoughts and feelings in written form, so the range of reflection will vary. In journal entries students will discuss how they went about finding a resource and how easy or difficult the search was. We ask them to think about what the resource did or did not do toward answering their research question. Experience has shown that because it is a required part of the project, students who find it difficult to put their experience in writing will eventually visit the instructor for some help and guidance. After the verbal discussion the instructor might say, "Okay, right now, write down some notes about this visit with me as one of your journal entries. What happened here? How do you feel? What decisions did you make about the research?" Explain that these are the kinds of comments the instructor expects to see in the journal entries for the project.

Some students will discover that they enjoy the challenge of academic research. Others will hate the amount of effort and time necessary to find their research sources. Some may simply provide declarative statements in their journals with no hint of the personal experiential journey. Encourage students to share their trials and tribulations. Be firm in your expectations for the research journal.

The journaling process allows students to articulate their research needs in an informal, reflective manner. Writing entries in research journals helps students develop their research ideas along the paper trail. Writing reflectively also highlights the similarities of the research process while students seek all formats and styles of information.

PART 3: ANNOTATED BIBLIOGRAPHY OF SOURCES USED

This piece addresses ACRL Standards 1, 2, 3, and 4.

This bibliography illustrates the student's ability to find, evaluate, and use information resources effectively. It teaches information gathering, evaluation, and presentation skills. While writing an annotated bibliography, students learn to find appropriate sources, to evaluate sources for usefulness to their projects, and finally to present the information in a concise format. All of these skills will play a major part in any research paper the student will have to produce in the future.

PART 4: ANNOTATED BIBLIOGRAPHY OF SOURCES NOT USED

This piece addresses ACRL Standards 1, 2, 3, and 4.

This bibliography emphasizes the student's skill in recognizing a source's faults or lack of relevance for a particular research question. It re-emphasizes the skills necessary for information gathering and evaluation, with a heavy focus on evaluation. Frequently, once students have located information related to a research topic, they are loathe to exclude it from the final work. This bibliography allows students to submit sources that seemed possibly helpful but didn't answer the research question because they didn't meet one or more of the evaluative criteria. This bibliography also provides practice in recognizing sources that may seem on topic, but ultimately fail the test of quality.

PART 5: PHYSICAL EXAMPLES OF THE RESEARCH

This piece addresses ACRL Standards 2, 3, and 4.

This part of the project is twofold. For the student, it teaches the importance of keeping a log or file of all research done from the preliminary foray to the end of the research process. For the instructor, having the physical examples of the research proves fairly well that students have not simply cut and pasted or plagiarized another's research into their own. We ask that all physical examples match the work submitted. This is not easy to do unless the student has actually done the research. Asking for the physical examples is well worth the time on the student's end as well as the extended amount of time needed to review the projects.

PART 6: MISCELLANEOUS RELEVANT SOURCES

This piece addresses ACRL Standards 2, 3, and 4.

This part of the Paper Trail Project teaches the value of information that isn't found strictly in books and journal articles. Many times research is influenced or directed by the invisible college of learners—fellow researchers and colleagues whom students communicate with informally during the research process. Student research can also be informed by physical and virtual materials provided by established organizations, associations, and institutions, experts in the field, and even other educators in higher education! For instance, some of the projects we have received have included physical items such as ballet shoes, performance videos, art works, music CDs, and documentary films. Others have included web links, electronic papers, and e-mail communications about works in progress.

METHODS OF FACILITATING THE PROJECT

The Paper Trail Project can be approached in several ways. It is most useful for an information literacy credit course or for use within a subject-specific course that has an integrated information literacy program. Using the exercises provided in this book, class time can be used to demonstrate, experience, and practice information literacy concepts involved in completing the Paper Trail Project. The project outlined in this book is based on the time allowed for a fifteen-week, three-credit course. When teaching time is more limited, the actual number of required sources for each of the bibliographies in the project may be reduced.

When time is limited, the Paper Trail Project can also be completed as a group collaboration. For a group project, the instructor should provide a generic research problem such as a local environmental issue or national current event. Small groups of students can work together to design an appropriate research question. If the small-group method is chosen, individual students would write the research journal entries for the parts of the research that they themselves had worked on, or the group might create a journal entry together.

In the optimal situation, all students should have enough time during the project to practice their information literacy skills by doing an exercise or homework assignment that demonstrates each of the project parts. This provides the opportunity for instructor feedback and student revisions before the project is completed.

Students sometimes delay creating a research question, even after searching, evaluating, and researching a topic for several weeks. Students sometimes are so enamored of their research question that they shy away from amending or modifying it to make it usable. Instructors must set a point, such as a research-question decision-deadline date, by which the research question must be designed, discussed, and approved by the instructor. It is only then that students can be assigned to continue to work on the Paper Trail Project.

Whether individual students work on their own Paper Trail Project or it is done by a small collaborative group of students, the path is clearly set from the beginning. The student learns to articulate a research need and develop a research question that is effective and manageable. The student learns to gather a wide variety of high-quality relevant sources and evaluate them so they will help answer the research question. The student learns to present the information in an effective format.

INTRODUCING THE PAPER TRAIL PROJECT

Introduce this project early and refresh students' memories often.

Explain to students that the project is based primarily on the goals and objectives of being information-literate students: their ability to gather, evaluate, and effectively use the resources they provide in their projects. This project is both the documentation and the personal journey of a student through the experience of the research process. Students should be told that the process will be messy. This is expected and accepted because it reflects the true nature of research. The Paper Trail Project is a great opportunity for students to try methods out over a period of time—be it only a few weeks or an entire semester—often without the added pressures of having to complete the paper or project for a subject-based course.

Students may be overwhelmed with the immensity of the project. Explain that it will be done step-by-step with the instructor guiding and facilitating the class. The class will act as an informal support group as they progress through the assignments that lead up to the finished Paper Trail Project. In the end, most students are amazed by the amount of information they have gathered and the quality of the resources they have amassed for this project.

Students consider it strange to document the research process and *not* write the paper. Do all in your power to be clear that the *process* is the project, not the paper!

Project Presentation Formats

The Paper Trail Project is specifically designed without a prescribed presentation style or format parameters. There are many required components, but the manner in which students choose to present their project is purposely left open. The project should be clearly outlined and firm in its expectations while at the same time flexible enough to allow variations in format.

Most students find that the traditional three-ring binder format with page separators works for them because it is a comfortable and familiar format. However, depending on the research project, it is conceivable that many other formats would work. Other formats that could be considered are web pages, PowerPoint presentations, student-created videos, and personal presentations. Of course, there are time limitations, and these must be considered by the instructor when suggesting acceptable formats. Allowing flexibility in presentation format leaves room for creativity and for accommodation of multiple learning styles.

Tips for Guiding Students through the Project

The Paper Trail Project is meant to teach students effective and reliable methods to use as they proceed through college-level research. At the same time, it exposes the side trips that occur while one is involved in research. So a benefit of the Paper Trail Project is that instructors can easily intervene to help students stay on track and remain successful.

Instructors can help students during the semester by guiding their progress toward completion of this project. Here is a list of possible suggestions to follow:

- On quizzes and tests, include an extra-credit question that might ask students to describe the point they have reached in researching their Paper Trail Project, or tell how they are feeling about the research process and the Paper Trail Project.

- Each Paper Trail Project exercise or assignment that will eventually end up as a part of the Paper Trail could be printed on the same color photocopy paper or have an identifying header on the page to alert students to its importance.

- Remind students of your office hours, send out e-mail notices, and mention it in class.

- At midsemester and again closer toward the end of the semester (adjust according to your time frame), hold an outside-of-class workshop for students who want to bring in their "stuff" for advice and help.

- Require that each student schedule a fifteen-minute meeting with you to discuss progress. You can make this graded or nongraded, but usually "mandatory" is enough to get them to come visit you.

- Provide several examples of past Paper Trail Projects and bring these to the classroom, put them on reserve in your library, or keep them available in your office. (Note: Be sure to get student authors' permission before you do this.)

The project design generally protects students from mediocrity or failure. However, instructors should be prepared for last minute realizations such as "I just realized I've been heading in the wrong direction for weeks!" "I just found a gold mine in a slightly different vein," or "This topic is killing me, I really need help!" These are natural occurrences and this project encourages them to be seen as part of the learning experience.

A class web page, a class discussion list, personal consultation, and individual e-mails can all be used to work with students while they travel the paper trail. There are students who will appear to breeze through the project, and for them the project is good practice for learning college-level research tools. There are also students who do not seem to have the "can-do" attitude or the creativity to complete this project. Perhaps these are the students who benefit most from the structure and support of the Paper Trail Project. Information literacy, a goal for lifelong learners and considered a new liberal art by many, is worth a little cheerleading.

GRADING

If used as the culminating project for a credit course, we recommend a very high weighted grade of 25 to 30 percent. Remind students that the grade is based on a series of assignments that they will have already had ample opportunity to practice and revise.

Grading Criteria for the Paper Trail Project

Keen attention to each part is necessary for successful completion of the project. Should a student overlook or skim lightly the work required for even one section, it will seriously impact the total work of the project. By providing a rubric for the students, everyone is clear as to what the expectations are and how they may attain the grade they desire.

Tips on Using the Grading Criteria

Provide clear criteria so that both student and instructor understand exactly what has been agreed on for the project requirements. Explain what the project must include to be successful in fulfilling its six parts. Tell students how they can earn a desired grade for their work.

As stated in the beginning of this chapter, the overall goal of the project is not simply a grade, but for students to learn to understand information concepts and to explore the information world through information gathering, evaluation, and presentation. Keeping that in mind, what is most important to the grade? The overall integrity and quality of the research are the most important attributes to look for when grading. Grading Paper Trail Projects must be done based on the known integrity of the student's process and the quality of the sources discovered, but not on whether the research question was perfectly or completely answered. Many students falsely believe that they should be able to solve all of their academic questions and completely answer all of the research issues they address. Allowing students to focus on the research process and stay true to the best evidence they can find will produce students who can pursue high-quality research and researchers who will stay lifelong learners.

STUDENT PAPER TRAIL EXAMPLE

TOPIC: PARASOCIAL INTERACTION

ENCYCLOPEDIA CITATION

"Parasocial Interaction." *A Dictionary of Communication and Media Studies*. 4th ed. New York: Hodder Headline Group, 1997.

ENCYCLOPEDIA ANNOTATION

The excerpt that I found from the *Dictionary of Communication and Media Studies* gave a basic definition of the term parasocial relationship. What I learned from it is that it is an illusion of an interpersonal relationship between a medium and an audience member. The medium can be television, computer, radio, or film. Long-running TV series are most often the cause of parasocial relationships, because the audience is allowed to grow up with the characters and learn everything about them. The relationships are unchanging and very comfortable.

ENCYCLOPEDIA RESEARCH JOURNAL ENTRY

I must say that when I picked this topic, I had no idea that it was going to be the most difficult thing ever. I had the hardest time trying to locate an encyclopedia article that had anything to do with my topic. At first I thought that it might be something new to the communication field, but as I did more research I found that the idea developed in the 1950s. I have tried many times to locate an encyclopedia, and I even went back to the computers every time I thought of a new search statement, but still no luck. I enclosed the page from the HELIN catalog that I got from using Encyclopedia and Parasocial Relationships, but since none of them related to my topic, I ended up using a dictionary. The information that I found in the dictionary was actually very helpful, and just like an encyclopedia would have done, it gave me some basic information and a really great place to start from.

CONCEPT MAP

What do I know about parasocial relationships? (See figure 9-1 for the concept map for the Paper Trail Project.)

RESEARCH QUESTION DEVELOPMENT

What are parasocial relationships?

What is parasocial interaction?

How do parasocial relationships or parasocial interaction relate to interpersonal communication?

What is the broad understanding of the term communication?

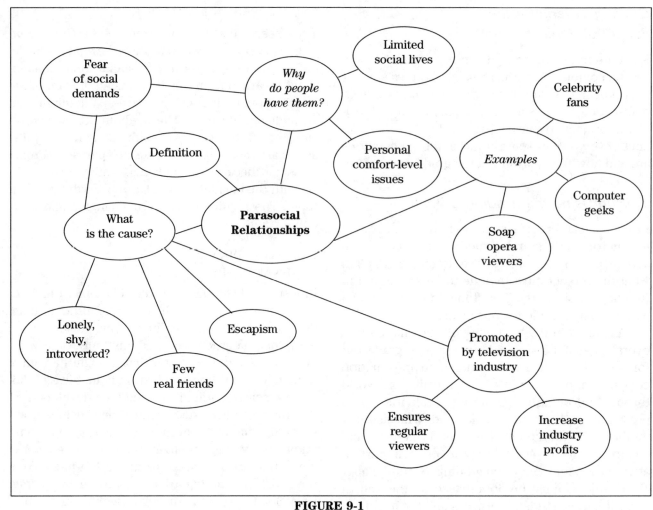

FIGURE 9-1
Concept Map for Parasocial Relationships

How does parasocial behavior impact communication skills?

Finalized question: How do parasocial relationships relate to interpersonal communication?

ANNOTATED BIBLIOGRAPHY OF SOURCES USED

Book

Fuller, Linda K. *Media-Mediated Relationships: Straight or Gay, Mainstream and Alternative Perspectives.* New York: Haworth Press, 1996.

Linda Fuller has a Ph.D. in communication and has written many other books in the field. She is a professor at Worcester State University and has taught in Singapore. Her book is very interesting to look at because of the many charts and graphs as well as footnotes that really help explain difficult wording. There are also commentaries written by other scholars at the beginning of the book that explain what a great book this is for college students who are trying to learn about media-mediated relationships (those based on a television show, movie, computer program, and so on). Since the book is fairly recent, there is a lot of very useful and up-to-date information that is mostly fact based, with a good addition of expert opinions to support it. The book seems easy to read because it is well-written and very organized. I did find some very good information about what it means to have a media-mediated relationship. I will be able to tie this into my topic because it explains the basis for parasocial interaction.

RESEARCH JOURNAL ENTRY

Basically, I had to do this the really hard way. I went onto the HELIN library catalog and was unable to find any books that had much to do with my topic (hence the printout of a search screen for a book that I didn't use). What I ended up doing (which ended up working out really well for me) was finding books that didn't really fit my topic and using them as a starting point. By locating books that *almost* fit my topic, I was in a section of the library where there were all sorts of other books about communication and the psychology of communication and interaction problems. I was able to physically look through books myself and find ones that I thought would be useful for explaining parasocial relationships. Since I wasn't quite sure about exactly what I needed, it was hard for me to tell the computer what to find. The more information I found, however, the easier it was to locate more.

Periodical

Rubin, Alan M. "Impact of Motivation, Attraction, and Parasocial Interaction on Talk-Radio Listening." *Journal of Broadcasting* 44, no. 4 (fall 2000): 635.

Alan Rubin has a Ph.D. in communication and is currently a professor at Kent State University. His article assumes that the reader has previous knowledge of the topic, so it is not intended for just the average reader. He seems to be writing for other people in the field who are familiar with certain language and processes. It was written in 2000, so the information is very up-to-date. It does contain a lot of opinion, but it is expert opinion. This article discusses parasocial relationships based on radio talk shows. It also explains a study that was done to find out who is most likely to form this kind of interaction. I am not as interested in this information as I have been with some of the other articles because its main focus is with radio and not with television. It does, however, give the best definition of parasocial interaction that I have come across so far.

RESEARCH JOURNAL ENTRY

At first I thought finding books was hard. Then I tried to find six articles on the topic of parasocial relationships, and I realized that finding books was a piece of cake. After spending a fairly decent amount of time at the URI Library (and turning up pretty empty handed), I decided to go to a place where things are just a little simpler. I went to the Greenville Public Library! I looked at print indexes there to find any articles related to my topic and I actually thought that it was a lot easier to use than the computer system. I know that I could have done the same thing at the URI Library, but my own public library is so much less intimidating, and I actually found two really great sources there. Once I thought of some new search words, I went back and looked for articles at URI and I was able to find more very useful things. The way that I was able to locate the articles that I needed was this— once I learned how to use the on-line databases with ease and accuracy I found that to be the best way. The most helpful database for my project was Com Abstracts, and that is where I found most of my articles. Once I found an article, I typed its title into the HELIN catalog and found out if it was bound or in the current periodicals room. I then went on a merry little search to see if the article I needed was available, and sometimes it was. More often than not I had to go back to the computer to try to find another, but I never gave up hope. HELIN did not let me down (too often). If at first you don't succeed, try again!

Web Site

Nass, Clifford. Is Human-Computer Interaction Social or Parasocial? August 1994. Stanford U. May 6, 2001. (http://www.stanford.edu/group/commdept/oldstuff/srct_pages/Social-Parasocial.html-40k)

This web site wasn't quite as interesting as some of the others, but it was pretty helpful. In the class that I actually had to write this paper for, Communications 103: Interpersonal Communications, I was supposed to relate parasocial interaction to computer stuff because it was an on-line class. The information I found here really helped me to tie in the other information I have to the computers. It was very easy to read and it was also helpful that it was very well organized. The references everywhere made the reading a little confusing, but Nass was still able to get his ideas across in an understandable way. I believe that he must be a credible scholar because his paper was submitted to the journal *Human Communication Research.*

RESEARCH JOURNAL ENTRY

Finding web sites was probably the easiest part of this project. It was even better because I could do it right from home. I am not going to lie to you, it was sometimes a real pain to have to drive all the way to Kingston just to photocopy a few pages from a book. Oh, well. So this was pretty cool. I just typed in some of my best search words and crossed my fingers. I had to evaluate every site that I found, but it was pretty easy to tell what was good, right from the opening of the page. I am finally becoming more comfortable with this topic because I am finding information—and the more I find, the more I want to keep looking. It's like finding that first tiny piece of gold. Miss Mary Mac, I actually did a lot more of this project along the way than I thought I did! Thanks for the help and advice.—Sandy.

ANNOTATED BIBLIOGRAPHY
OF SOURCES NOT USED

Web Example

Sturdy, John C. G. The Church as a Parasocial Framework. (http://www.cb1.com/~john/Religion/index.html) Accessed April 24, 2001.

I thought that it might be interesting to get a different perspective on this by looking at the religious point of view. Well, this web site was no good. Beside the fact that it is a very uninteresting web site to look at, the links don't really lead anywhere helpful, and the information is not what I am looking for. Oh, well, it was a nice try.

Physical Examples of Materials

Here is a list of the assortment of items that one would include: search screen printouts from catalogs, databases, web search engines and directo-ries, printouts of the title pages of resources used, brochures, maps, newsletters, photographs, pamphlets and any physical items that support the research done.

Expert Information

David C. Giles, Coventry University, School of Health and Social Sciences, Psychology, Coventry University, Priory Street, Coventry, UK CV1. Telephone (UK) 024-7688 7688 Telephone (International) +44 24 7688 7688 (http://www.hss.coventry.ac.uk/psychology/giles.htm) Accessed May 6, 2002.

Giles' research interests are as follows: "My main interests lie in the psychology of the media and in developmental psychology. What I am particularly interested in is the phenomenon of 'parasocial interaction' by which people build up relationships with media figures (for example, celebrities). I am currently trying to develop a general theory of parasocial interaction which accounts for different types of media figures and different media."

RESEARCH JOURNAL ENTRY

OK, so at this point I am wicked stressed out. You would think that I would have learned my lesson after not handing in those class reading response essays on time, but I didn't. I waited until tonight (the day before the project is due!) to find an expert. I actually found someone I think would be a really good source considering his credentials, but, of course, there is no way to reach him at this point. The thing that bothers me the most about this is that for once I have actually worked on something for a long time. I really didn't wait until the night before to do the whole project, and I was feeling good about that until I realized that I forgot to find and contact an expert.

The only thing that makes me feel even a little bit better, is that I know that I worked really hard on this project. I chose one of the hardest topics, and although there were times when I wanted to give up on it, I didn't. After sticking with and learning about different ways to do things, I believe that it turned out pretty well. If not, at least I have some really great new information about how to do a great paper every time. And, by the way, I did do really well on my COM103 paper; all of this work did pay off in the end, so maybe I shouldn't feel so discouraged. On the other hand, I need to stop being such a procrastinator!

I am finally done! OK, so it wasn't that bad, but toward the end I just started getting tired of doing the same thing over and over again. I must, however, say that I did learn a lot from this project, because I always assumed that I knew how to do really great research. Boy, was I ever wrong. I think that the last time I ever used a book or an encyclopedia as a source for a paper was junior high. I am really glad that I know what to do now, and I think my professor will be really excited to see all of the different kinds of sources that I used. I have already done two other papers using some of the methods I have learned along the way, and they have come out a lot better than anything I would have done before. So, you win—it was worth it. Thank you—Sandy Clossick

P.S. Thanks from all of my future professors who will possibly be receiving quality work from now on!

STUDENT TIME LINE FOR COMPLETING THE PAPER TRAIL PROJECT

This time line is based on implementing the Paper Trail Project during a fifteen-week information literacy course.

Week 1: General Introduction to the Paper Trail Project

In class: Discuss Paper Trail Project goal and objectives.

Receive handout describing the requirements for the project.

Out of class: Students brainstorm and jot down ideas that can be developed into topics for their Paper Trail Projects.

Week 2: Choosing a Topic

In class: Students identify and locate encyclopedias during class time.

Students use instructor-provided guide to practice writing encyclopedia citation and annotation.

Students receive instruction on how to write research journal entries.

Out of class: Students find an encyclopedia article on their topic, create a citation and annotation for the article, and write a research journal entry about the process.

Week 3: Developing the Research Question

In class: Students create a concept map for their topic.

Students use worksheets to develop possible Paper Trail research questions.

Out of class: Students develop finalized Paper Trail Project research questions and write a research journal entry on the process.

Week 4: Finding and Using Books

In class: Students search the catalog and retrieve books relevant to their topics.

Week 5: Developing an Annotated Bibliography of Books

In class: Using instructor-provided guide and verbal instructions, students learn to prepare formal Annotated Bibliography of Books.

Out of class: Students complete a five-item Annotated Bibliography of Books, writing research journal entries for each item.

Week 6: Finding and Using Print Periodical Literature

In class: Students practice using print indexes to identify citations.

Students practice locating articles using the library catalog.

Out of class: Students identify, read, and evaluate several periodical articles from print indexes for their Paper Trail Projects.

Week 7: Finding and Using Electronic Periodical Literature

In class: Students practice using on-line periodical databases to identify relevant periodical citations for their Paper Trail Projects.

Students practice using evaluative criteria to judge the appropriateness of articles for their projects.

Out of class: Students use electronic periodical databases to identify and locate five relevant articles on their Paper Trail topic.

Week 8: Developing an Annotated Bibliography of Articles

In class: Using the guide provided, students practice writing periodical citations and annotations.

Out of class: Students develop and write a five-item Annotated Bibliography of Periodical Articles on their topic and include research journal entries for each.

Week 9: Using Experts and Statistics in Research

In class: Students practice using library tools to identify experts and statistics on their topics.

Out of class: Students identify and contact three experts asking for information for their research.

Students identify and cite three supportive statistics for their Paper Trail Project.

Students write research journal entries for "Experts and Statistics."

Week 10: Finding Web Sites for Research

In class: Students practice using effective web searching techniques to find quality web sites related to their topics.

Out of class: Students select several web sites and describe their content and usefulness in journal entries.

Students continue to identify, obtain, and evaluate relevant books, articles, expert information, statistics, and web sites and comment on what they have found in their journal entries.

Week 11: Evaluating Web Sites for Research

In class: Students evaluate their selected web sites based on criteria discussed in class.

Students practice writing citations and annotations for web sites.

Out of class: Students develop and write a five-item Annotated Bibliography of Web Sites including research journal entries for each web site used.

Week 12: Putting It All Together

In class: Students meet with instructor to review Paper Trail Project progress.

Out of class: Students revise, update, and complete Paper Trail Project parts.

Weeks 13 and 14: Putting It All Together

Out of class: Students complete and finalize projects outside of class.

Students contact instructor via e-mail or phone for guidance.

Week 15: Paper Trail Project Completed

In class: All projects turned in today!

Information Literacy Competency Standards for Higher Education

STANDARD ONE
The information literate student determines the nature and extent of the information needed.

Performance Indicators

PART 1. The information literate student defines and articulates the need for information.

OUTCOMES INCLUDE

Confers with instructors and participates in class discussions, peer workgroups, and electronic discussions to identify a research topic or other information need

Develops a thesis statement and formulates questions based on the information need

Explores general information sources to increase familiarity with the topic

Defines or modifies the information need to achieve a manageable focus

Identifies key concepts and terms that describe the information need

Recognizes that existing information can be combined with original thought, experimentation, and/or analysis to produce new information

PART 2. The information literate student identifies a variety of types and formats of potential sources for information.

OUTCOMES INCLUDE

Knows how information is formally and informally produced, organized, and disseminated

Recognizes that knowledge can be organized into disciplines that influence the way information is accessed

Identifies the value and differences of potential resources in a variety of formats (e.g., multimedia, database, website, data set, audio/visual, book)

Identifies the purpose and audience of potential resources (e.g., popular vs. scholarly, current vs. historical)

Differentiates between primary and secondary sources, recognizing how their use and importance vary with each discipline

Realizes that information may need to be constructed with raw data from primary sources

PART 3. The information literate student considers the costs and benefits of acquiring the needed information.

OUTCOMES INCLUDE

Determines the availability of needed information and makes decisions on broadening the information-seeking process beyond local resources (e.g., interlibrary loan; using resources at other locations; obtaining images, videos, text, or sound)

Considers the feasibility of acquiring a new language or skill (e.g., foreign or discipline-based) in order to gather needed information and to understand its context

Defines a realistic overall plan and time line to acquire the needed information

Association of College and Research Libraries, Information Literacy Competency Standards for Higher Education, Standards, Performance Indicators, and Outcomes. Approved by ACRL Board, January 18, 2000

PART 4. The information literate student reevaluates the nature and extent of the information need.

OUTCOMES INCLUDE

Reviews the initial information need to clarify, revise, or refine the question

Describes criteria used to make information decisions and choices

STANDARD TWO
The information literate student accesses needed information effectively and efficiently.

Performance Indicators

PART 1. The information literate student selects the most appropriate investigative methods or information retrieval systems for accessing the needed information.

OUTCOMES INCLUDE

Identifies appropriate investigative methods (e.g., laboratory experiment, simulation, fieldwork)

Investigates benefits and applicability of various investigative methods

Investigates the scope, content, and organization of information retrieval systems

Selects efficient and effective approaches for accessing the information needed from the investigative method or information retrieval system

PART 2. The information literate student constructs and implements effectively designed search strategies.

OUTCOMES INCLUDE

Develops a research plan appropriate to the investigative method

Identifies keywords, synonyms, and related terms for the information needed

Selects controlled vocabulary specific to the discipline or information retrieval source

Constructs a search strategy using appropriate commands for the information retrieval system selected (e.g., Boolean operators, truncation, and proximity for search engines; internal organizers such as indexes for books)

Implements the search strategy in various information retrieval systems using different user interfaces and search engines, with different command languages, protocols, and search parameters

Implements the search using investigative protocols appropriate to the discipline

PART 3. The information literate student retrieves information on-line or in person using a variety of methods.

OUTCOMES INCLUDE

Uses various search systems to retrieve information in a variety of formats

Uses various classification schemes and other systems (e.g., call number systems or indexes) to locate information resources within the library or to identify specific sites for physical exploration

Uses specialized online or in person services available at the institution to retrieve information needed (e.g., interlibrary loan/document delivery, professional associations, institutional research offices, community resources, experts and practitioners)

Uses surveys, letters, interviews, and other forms of inquiry to retrieve primary information

PART 4. The information literate student refines the search strategy if necessary.

OUTCOMES INCLUDE

Assesses the quantity, quality, and relevance of the search results to determine whether alternative information retrieval systems or investigative methods should be utilized

Identifies gaps in the information retrieved and determines if the search strategy should be revised

Repeats the search using the revised strategy as necessary

PART 5. The information literate student extracts, records, and manages the information and its sources.

OUTCOMES INCLUDE

Selects among various technologies the most appropriate one for the task of extracting the needed information (e.g., copy/paste software functions, photocopier, scanner, audio/visual equipment, or exploratory instruments)

Creates a system for organizing the information

Differentiates between the types of sources cited and understands the elements and correct syntax of a citation for a wide range of resources

Records all pertinent citation information for future reference

Uses various technologies to manage the information selected and organized

STANDARD THREE
The information literate student evaluates information and its sources critically and incorporates selected information into his or her knowledge base and value system.

Performance Indicators

PART 1. The information literate student summarizes the main ideas to be extracted from the information gathered.

OUTCOMES INCLUDE

Reads the text and selects main ideas

Restates textual concepts in his/her own words and selects data accurately

Identifies verbatim material that can be then appropriately quoted

PART 2. The information literate student articulates and applies initial criteria for evaluating both the information and its sources.

OUTCOMES INCLUDE

Examines and compares information from various sources in order to evaluate reliability, validity, accuracy, authority, timeliness, and point of view or bias

Analyzes the structure and logic of supporting arguments or methods

Recognizes prejudice, deception, or manipulation

Recognizes the cultural, physical, or other context within which the information was created and understands the impact of context on interpreting the information

PART 3. The information literate student synthesizes main ideas to construct new concepts.

OUTCOMES INCLUDE

Recognizes interrelationships among concepts and combines them into potentially useful primary statements with supporting evidence

Extends initial synthesis, when possible, at a higher level of abstraction to construct new hypotheses that may require additional information

Utilizes computer and other technologies (e.g., spreadsheets, databases, multimedia, and audio or visual equipment) for studying the interaction of ideas and other phenomena

PART 4. The information literate student compares new knowledge with prior knowledge to determine the value added, contradictions, or other unique characteristics of the information.

OUTCOMES INCLUDE

Determines whether information satisfies the research or other information need

Uses consciously selected criteria to determine whether the information contradicts or verifies information used from other sources

Draws conclusions based upon information gathered

Tests theories with discipline-appropriate techniques (e.g., simulators, experiments)

Determines probable accuracy by questioning the source of the data, the limitations of the information gathering tools or strategies, and the reasonableness of the conclusions

Integrates new information with previous information or knowledge

Selects information that provides evidence for the topic

PART 5. The information literate student determines whether the new knowledge has an impact on the individual's value system and takes steps to reconcile differences.

OUTCOMES INCLUDE

Investigates differing viewpoints encountered in the literature

Determines whether to incorporate or reject viewpoints encountered

PART 6. The information literate student validates understanding and interpretation of the information through discourse with other individuals, subject-area experts, and/or practitioners.

OUTCOMES INCLUDE

Participates in classroom and other discussions

Participates in class-sponsored electronic communication forums designed to encourage discourse on the topic (e.g., e-mail, bulletin boards, chat rooms)

Seeks expert opinion through a variety of mechanisms (e.g., interviews, e-mail, listservs)

PART 7. The information literate student determines whether the initial query should be revised.

OUTCOMES INCLUDE

Determines if original information need has been satisfied or if additional information is needed

Reviews search strategy and incorporates additional concepts as necessary

Reviews information retrieval sources used and expands to include others as needed

STANDARD FOUR
The information literate student, individually or as a member of a group, uses information effectively to accomplish a specific purpose.

Performance Indicators

PART 1. The information literate student applies new and prior information to the planning and creation of a particular product or performance.

OUTCOMES INCLUDE

Organizes the content in a manner that supports the purposes and format of the product or performance (e.g., outlines, drafts, storyboards)

Articulates knowledge and skills transferred from prior experiences to planning and creating the product or performance

Integrates the new and prior information, including quotations and paraphrasings, in a manner that supports the purposes of the product or performance

Manipulates digital text, images, and data, as needed, transferring them from their original locations and formats to a new context

PART 2. The information literate student revises the development process for the product or performance.

OUTCOMES INCLUDE

Maintains a journal or log of activities related to the information seeking, evaluating, and communicating process

Reflects on past successes, failures, and alternative strategies

PART 3. The information literate student communicates the product or performance effectively to others.

OUTCOMES INCLUDE

Chooses a communication medium and format that best supports the purposes of the product or performance and the intended audience

Uses a range of information technology applications in creating the product or performance

Incorporates principles of design and communication

Communicates clearly and with a style that supports the purposes of the intended audience

STANDARD FIVE
The information literate student understands many of the economic, legal, and social issues surrounding the use of information and accesses and uses information ethically and legally.

Performance Indicators

PART 1. The information literate student understands many of the ethical, legal and socio-economic issues surrounding information and information technology.

OUTCOMES INCLUDE

Identifies and discusses issues related to privacy and security in both the print and electronic environments

Identifies and discusses issues related to free vs. fee-based access to information

Identifies and discusses issues related to censorship and freedom of speech

Demonstrates an understanding of intellectual property, copyright, and fair use of copyrighted material

PART 2. The information literate student follows laws, regulations, institutional policies, and etiquette related to the access and use of information resources.

OUTCOMES INCLUDE

Participates in electronic discussions following accepted practices (e.g., "Netiquette")

Uses approved passwords and other forms of ID for access to information resources

Complies with institutional policies on access to information resources

Preserves the integrity of information resources, equipment, systems and facilities

Legally obtains, stores, and disseminates text, data, images, or sounds

Demonstrates an understanding of what constitutes plagiarism and does not represent work attributable to others as his/her own

Demonstrates an understanding of institutional policies related to human subjects research

PART 3. The information literate student acknowledges the use of information sources in communicating the product or performance.

OUTCOMES INCLUDE

Selects an appropriate documentation style and uses it consistently to cite sources

Posts permission granted notices, as needed, for copyrighted material

For more complete information please go to: www. ala.org/acrl/ilcomstan.html

APPENDIX B ▶▶▶▶▶▶▶▶▷ For Further Reading

There are dozens of web-mounted gateways that lead the researcher to abundant and uniformly good publications, resources, links to other sites, and programs of all kinds. Listed below are just a few sites that will connect the interested instructor to a wealth of ideas and information.

AMERICAN COLLEGE AND RESEARCH LIBRARIES. 2002.

Information Literacy Web Page
   Available at: http://www.ala.org/acrl/il/index. html
   Accessed on 1-2-03.

This site is a gateway to and a gathering place for resources on information literacy focused on improving the teaching, learning, and research role of the higher education community.

BREIVIK, PATRICIA SENN, CHAIR. 2002.

The National Forum on Information Literacy Publications Section
   Available at: http://www. infolit.org/

This web site lists links to organizations, publications, conferences, and other information literacy related subjects.

EISENBERG, MIKE, AND BOB BERKOWITZ

The Big Six: Information Literacy for the Information Age
   Available at: www.big6.com/
   Accessed 1-2-03.

Information related to teaching information literacy skills to children in elementary and secondary education, including lessons, links, research, and resources.

SHAPIRO, JEREMEY J., AND SHELLEY K. HUGHES. 1996.

Information Literacy as a Liberal Art. Educom Review 31(2)
   Available at: http://www.educause.edu/pub/ er/review/reviewArticles/31231.html
   Accessed 2-2-03.

View from the education community on the needs of today's students.

SMITH, DREW, EDITOR. 2002.

Directory of Online Resources for Information Literacy
   Available at: http://www.cas.usf.edu/ lis/il/
   Accessed 1-2-03

This comprehensive on-line directory includes a wide variety of information on information literacy under the headings: Assessment, Bibliographies and Webographies, Conferences, Definitions, Electronic Mailing Lists, The Information Literacy Process, Organizations and Projects, Papers and Presentations, Programs in Higher Education, Programs in K-12 Education, and Tutorials.

▶▶▶▶▶▶▶▶ INDEX

planning of research. *See* Research
    process
point of view, 12–13
preservation, 46–47
primary sources
    definition, 8–9
    types of information (exercise 5), 11
privacy of information, 43, 44
    on Internet (exercise 17), 44, 45
    privacy (exercise 18), 44, 46
procrastination, 17, 89, 90
Project Gutenberg, 76
proprietary information, availability of,
    74, 76
publications, type of, and evaluation,
    13
publishers and publishing, 40
purpose of information, 77. *See also*
    Information needs

Q
quality of information, 12
    periodicals, 59–61
    quality of information (exercise 6),
        13–15
    and self-published materials, 40
quoting. *See* Plagiarism

R
relevancy of information, 12–13
reliability of information, 77
research journal in Paper Trail Project,
    87–88
research methods, development of,
    33–35
research process, 17–31
    analogies (exercise 7), 17–18, 19
    concept mapping (exercise 9), 21,
        23–24
    disciplines and subject areas (exer-
        cise 10), 25–26
    encyclopedias/background informa-
        tion, 18, 21, 22
    formulating a research question
        (exercise 11), 27–28

handout, 20
and Paper Trail Project, 87, 89–90
search terms (exercise 12), 29–31
research questions
    brainstorming on, 23
    changing research topics, 25
    narrowing a topic (exercise 11),
        27–28
    statement of research topic, 21
restricting a topic (exercise 11), 27–28

S
scholarly literature in information
    cycle, 33
scientific information and authorship, 38
search engines
    operation of, 73
    vs. periodical databases (exercise
        31), 73–74, 75
    as research tools, 72
search statements
    formulation of, 66
    search statements (exercise 29),
        66–67
search strategies
    Internet, 74, 76
    statistics, 82
search terms (exercise 12), 29–31
secondary sources, 8–9
sources of information. *See*
    Information sources
specialization in information retrieval,
    1–2
statement of research topic, 21
*Statistical Abstract of the United
    States*, 84
    Statistical Abstract (exercise 35),
        84–85
statistics, 81–85
    search strategies, 82
    Statistical Abstract (exercise 35),
        84–85
    statistics (exercise 34), 82–83
    tools, 84–85
    types of, 81

structure of Internet sites, 77
subject headings (exercise 23), 53–54
subjective information, 8, 12–13
synonyms and key words, 27

T
technology and access to information,
    47
tertiary information, 8–9
time line for Paper Trail Project,
    95–96
time sensitivity of information
    and information cycle (exercise 13),
        33, 34
    and tools, 29
tools
    background information, 18,
        21, 22
    books, 48–58
    experts, 79, (exercise 33) 79–80
    indexes, 63–65
    Internet. *see* Internet
    organizations, 79, (exercise 33)
        79–80
    periodicals, 59–62
    statistics, 81–85
topics. *See* Research questions

U
U.S. government documents
    access to, 47
    as source of statistics, 84
usefulness of information. *See*
    Relevancy of information

W
Web. *See* Internet
Web directories (exercise 31),
    73–74
Web sites, preservation of, 47
Wilson indexes (exercise 28),
    63, 65
word search. *see* Key words
working papers, 59

Joanna M. Burkhardt is associate professor and head librarian at the University of Rhode Island (URI), Providence, where she also coordinates the information literacy program and teaches sections of URI's course in information literacy. She is an active member of the American Library Association (ALA), the Association of College and Research Libraries (ACRL), and the Rhode Island Library Association.

Mary C. MacDonald is an assistant professor in the reference unit of the library at the University of Rhode Island, Kingston, where she serves as the information literacy librarian and oversees the development of the information literacy program. She is an active member of ALA, ACRL, and the Rhode Island Library Association.

Andrée J. Rathemacher is an assistant professor in the reference unit of the library at the University of Rhode Island, Kingston, where she is the business specialist and bibliographer. She teaches in the library's information literacy program and has designed information literacy modules that have been integrated into the university curriculum. She is an active member of the ALA, ACRL, and the Rhode Island Library Association.

The authors were winners of the Outstanding Paper of the Year in *Reference Services Review* for the year 2000: "Challenges in building an incremental, multiyear information literacy plan," *RSR: Reference Services Review* 28(3) (2000): 240-47.